Tank Commander

Tank Commander

From the Cold War to the Gulf and Beyond

Stuart Crawford

Pen & Sword

MILITARY

AN IMPRINT OF PEN & SWORD BOOKS LTD.
YORKSHIRE - PHILADELPHIA

First published in Great Britain in 2023
by Pen & Sword Military
An imprint of
Pen & Sword Books Limited
Yorkshire - Philadelphia

ISBN 978 1 39908 229 7

A CIP catalogue record for this book is available from the British Library

Typeset in INDIA by IMPEC eSolutions
Printed and bound in the UK by CPI Group (UK) Ltd, Croydon, CRO 4YY

Pen & Sword Books Limited incorporates the imprints of Atlas, Archaeology, Aviation, Discovery, Family History, Fiction, History, Maritime, Military, Military Classics, Politics, Select, Transport, True Crime, Air World, Frontline Publishing, Leo Cooper, Remember When, Seaforth Publishing, The Praetorian Press, Wharncliffe Local History, Wharncliffe Transport, Wharncliffe True Crime and White Owl.

For a complete list of Pen & Sword titles please contact
PEN & SWORD BOOKS LIMITED
47 Church Street, Barnsley, South Yorkshire S70 2AS, United Kingdom
E-mail: enquiries@pen-and-sword.co.uk
Website: www.pen-and-sword.co.uk

Or

PEN AND SWORD BOOKS
1950 Lawrence Rd, Havertown, PA 19083, USA
E-mail: Uspen-and-sword@casematepublishers.com
Website: www.penandswordbooks.com

To India, Hector, and Millicent.
Lang may your lums reek!

Contents

Foreword

Stuart Crawford and I have been friends for approaching thirty years. It started as one of those fortuitous encounters which occur sometimes in life by blind chance. I'd been sent out to Germany as the Glasgow Herald's defence correspondent to tour various British bases in advance of the 1991 Gulf War. I wrote a piece saying we'd better hope the Russian hordes didn't surge across the Inner German Border anytime soon, since most of the UK's heavy military equipment appeared to have either already departed in the direction of Saudi Arabia or been seriously depleted.

Stuart promptly wrote a letter to the editor saying his regiment – 4th Royal Tanks – was still in position holding the line for NATO. It was just that the unit's tanks were short of a few engines, gear-boxes and gun-barrels, not to mention much of their ammunition. All had been looted mercilessly to provide spares and reserves for 1 (UK) Armoured Division, then en route for, or assembling in, the Middle East. His sense of humour appealed to me and I determined to meet him as soon as practicable after the war. I then deployed for the next six months to the sandy wastes.

We also had a mutual friend, the late Colonel Clive Fairweather, who at that time was the longest-serving surviving

SAS officer in uniform. I'd known Clive from Northern Ireland days, when he commanded the Hereford Hooligan detachment in the province from Bessbrook Mill in the bandit country of South Armagh. In future years, we three would meet regularly for rather liquid lunches in Edinburgh's Doric Tavern and for banter which firmly cemented our friendship.

The British military is a relatively small organisation and our paths had also crossed on several occasions pre- and post-Gulf War. On a facility visit to Cyprus, I was assigned Stuart's room in the headquarters at Dhekelia while he was on leave. He had even been kind enough to leave me several of the biggest cockroaches I'd ever encountered until then to share the accommodation in case I wearied for company.

My own bona fides for being invited to pen this foreword were thirty plus years' experience covering conflicts across the globe. The first was the long war in Northern Ireland from the early 1970s onwards. Since most of my maternal family hail from the province and I'd spent a lot of childhood holidays up in the Antrim Glens and in the towns and cities, I was familiar with the geography, the issues and many of the players involved in that tragic sectarian clash. It was also useful knowledge when out with nocturnal army patrols in Belfast to be able to advise confused young subalterns peering forlornly at street maps in the darkness on the best and quickest route to be followed back to base.

Then it was the Falklands attached to Four-Five Commando, Royal Marines, for the landings and the 'yomp' across the islands. I was barely home a month when I was sent off to Lebanon to cover the multi-sided civil war raging there. The 1991 Gulf War and a six-month absence from home followed.

It was an experience of desert warfare which stood me in good stead for the next bout of unpleasantness in that region, bolted onto the Black Watch battlegroup, in 2003. In between, there were the various Balkan wars in Croatia, Bosnia and Kosovo and a fervent personal confirmation of Otto von Bismarck's opinion that the entire Balkans 'are not worth the life of a single Pomeranian grenadier'.

There were some in the military and defence establishment who regarded Stuart as a 'maverick', even after he was groomed for higher command by attendance at the prestigious British and American staff colleges. That's usually a prerequisite for those deemed to be potential high flyers. But while it's true that he did not necessarily toe the party line, that, I feel certain, was more because of his innate professional and personal honesty rather than from any inclination to be seen as a rebel.

That honesty shines through in the book, where he also answers candidly the frequently asked civilian question of what professional soldiers do when they're not involved in war or serious training. Pre the Iraq and Afghanistan merry-go-round deployments of the past two decades, professional soldiers often spent their entire careers without hearing a shot fired in anger. Many were based for years in Germany with British Army of the Rhine, training for a war most hoped would never happen and which they knew they were unlikely to survive if it did. A senior general once admitted to me in confidence that if the Soviet Third Guards Shock Army and its Warsaw Pact allies ever struck west, BAOR would be little more than a speed-bump in their path. 'Oh, we'd make their eyes water, but they'd punch through and we'd cease to exist as an army,' he said.

Given the tensions and uncertainties of the Cold War, the lengthy periods between small-unit drills and large exercises involved a lot of boredom. When the real-life tedium of administrative niff-naff collides with a body of fit, well-trained professionals facing the potential carnage of a Cold War turned hot, the outcome often manifests itself in heavy drinking, fast cars or motorbikes and occasionally perilous merry japes, all of which are dealt with in often amusing detail in this volume.

More seriously, Stuart's account of British headquarters in Riyadh during the 1991 Iraq war rings many familiar and disquieting bells. Information and intelligence once the ground phase of the fighting began was sketchy or non-existent. Pressured by the authorities back in the UK for situation updates, there was frequently little or nothing for high command to impart. Communications between front-line units in the desert and headquarters were intermittent at best and frequently a shambles. It had shades of the 1999 invasion of Kosovo, where the immensely expensive British Bowman digital radio comms system simply failed to function and ground commanders were reduced to using personal and hugely insecure cellphones to pass orders to their units.

There is also the question of British commanders being slow to exploit success and reluctant to take tactical decisions which might result in politically-embarrassing casualties, particularly when contrasted with the flexibility and drive of their US counterparts. The Great British Public has become intolerant of battlefield losses in the last few decades. It is an attitude which is now apparently an ingrained political as well as military maxim to the detriment of all concerned. But in any case, with a much-diminished army in terms of manpower and tanks, it would appear unlikely that Britain could field and sustain anything beyond a brigade in any future conflict without a major uptick in funding and equipment. Even then, it would take years to bring new forces to the necessary levels of competence and professionalism.

For anyone wishing a candid, warts-and-all account of peacetime military life, this book is as good as you'll find. Written with unvarnished honesty and an all-pervading humour, it covers all of the essentials and much more controversial ground than military authors are usually wont to reveal. It's a thoroughly enjoyable and informative read, from the serious but inevitably flawed business of running a headquarters in war to the ludicrous reality of losing a fifty-six tonne tank after a major exercise, only to have it reappear six weeks later tucked away in a French railway siding, or having young officers riding a motorbike up the stairs of the officers' mess and over their sleeping comrades on the upper floor. It was ever thus, probably even before Centurion was a rank rather than a tank.

Ian Bruce
Former defence correspondent, the Glasgow Herald.

Chapter 1

As far back as I can remember, I always wanted to be a soldier. I can't really explain why, it's just the way it was. My Dad had been subaltern in the Highland Light Infantry (HLI) just after the Second World War when he did his National Service and had always spoken fondly of his time in uniform, but we weren't a military family in the classic sense. I was just born with it I guess, just as other folk are born to be trainspotters or stamp collectors. Whatever floats your boat.

In common with other families in Britain, though, there was a strong thread of military service running through my family. My grandfather, Charles Marshall Crawford, was a schoolteacher born in 1889 and brought up in the village of Carmunnock, then in Lanarkshire now in the City of Glasgow, who had volunteered (as you did in the First World War) with all his local pals and joined the Royal Army Medical Corps (RAMC). His unit, in which he reached the rank of corporal, was sent out to Italy in a little known episode in the struggle against Germany and the Austro-Hungarian Empire.

In later life he used to sit out in the sun in East Kilbride, where he lived latterly, with his peer group friends, one of whom had been bayoneted on the Somme but had survived. I got little out of him about his army service, save that he had been present at the Battle of Caporetto (12th Isonzo) in 1917 where he claimed to have been 'the first man in the retreat' and where he commented that his Italian comrades had all thrown their rifles in the canal and run away. That and a tale where his unit had been billeted in a factory which 'they thought made lemonade' (aye, right) and where they slaked their thirst only to wake up in hospital several days later, so family legend has it. But he also had to hold a man down whilst the surgeon amputated his leg with a razor blade, which made him 'sick as a dog'.

My mother's elder brother, Victor Hawthorne, had also volunteered at the start of the Second World War on 3 September 1939, and off he went as a private soldier into the Royal Artillery (RA). He returned six years later as a staff captain with tuberculosis, and was one of the very first to be cured of this terrible affliction by the new drug penicillin. He was at the battles of Imphal and Kohima, which is about as serious soldiering in wartime as you can get. But once again I could get nothing much out of him, except the beginnings of a story where he said, 'So, the CO told me to take two Bren Carriers and clear this road'. 'What happened then?' I would say, eyes agog. 'Oh, you don't want to hear that old boring story', he would reply. And that was it. I never found out.

My Dad, Robert Crawford, was one of that generation of village boys who did everything well; they were good at football and golf, they could dance, they could play musical instruments, they could draw and paint, and they could charm the girls. He had been a member of the Glasgow University Home Guard before being called up in 1945. I suspect he would have volunteered before that but his brother, Tom Crawford, the uncle I never met, had died on active service, but not in combat, on 9 July 1944 whilst a Lance-Bombardier in a light anti-aircraft regiment in Kent before deployment to France. Dad said that his mother never recovered from the shock and I guess that probably stopped him volunteering before his call up.

He was eventually called up with his peer group, and famously arrived at Catterick Station in Yorkshire for basic military training to be greeted by the headlines on the station platform 'Japan Surrenders'. Nonetheless he soldiered on, and after six weeks of square bashing was called into the company commander's office and told that he really should attend a War Office Selection Board ('WOSBIE') and have a bash at becoming an officer. This he duly passed, and ended up at the Royal Military Academy, Sandhurst (RMAS), where the occupant of the next room to his was the duke of somewhere or other. That's Sandhurst for you, folks, it's the great social leveller.

He was due to join his battalion in Greece where they were fighting against the Greek People's Liberation Army (ELAS) which was effectively the military wing of the Greek Communist Party. However, the HLI had 'too many officers' and he was therefore sent to Palestine and attached to a Royal Army Ordnance Corps (RAOC) depot in Rafah on the Egyptian border. On arrival he was given his own batman, or officer's servant, as was the norm. His was a chap called Helmut (no surname remembered) who was ex-Afrika Korps and had been captured at El Alamein. Four years later and he had still to be repatriated.

My father spent two peaceful and relatively stress free years in Palestine, although the Jewish insurgent movement had declared a revolt against the British in 1944 and blew up a wing of the King

David Hotel in Jerusalem two years later, killing ninety-one and injuring forty-six more. In contrast, Dad's main claim to fame was to have designed a nine-hole golf course in the desert and been an eager participant in the competitive dinners hosted by all the officers' messes in the vicinity. The record number of courses served at any of these epicurean events was seventeen!

So I guess there was a tradition of military service of sorts in my background, but it was little different from any other families. Comics and Airfix models have to take part responsibility for my military fascination also though. My comic of choice growing up was the Victor, which majored on stories of derring-do in the military, from which I graduated to Commando comics. Almost all of the story lines were based in the war and presented in a very positive and gung-ho fashion. Whether Airfix arrived concurrently or later I can't quite remember, but again I graduated from early attempts at aeroplanes to tanks and armoured cars. I longed to visit the near-mythical Tank Museum at Bovington in Dorset, but it might as well have been on the moon as far as a Glasgow-based schoolboy enthusiast was concerned in those days.

I got there (both becoming a soldier and seeing the Tank Museum) in the end, but it took some time to achieve mind. School and university got in the way, then that splendid old-fashioned west coast Presbyterianism told me that I really should have a career to fall back on if my military aspirations came to naught. It just so happened that my degree in land economy exempted me from the examinations to qualify as a chartered surveyor, so I spent two years plus qualifying as that, most of it spent with the British Rail Property Board in their headquarters at the top of Buchanan Street in Glasgow. The day I qualified I decided to try and join the army, hoping to get a three year Short Service Commission (SSC) a bit like my Dad had done.

Up to this point I had no experience of the army whatsoever, not at school, not in the Combined Cadet Force (CCF), not in the Territorial Army (TA). I was truly a military virgin. But I did know a bit about universities, and I knew that Glasgow University (sorry, the University of Glasgow, I'll get it right next time) would have an army liaison office somewhere and, after a quick look through the Yellow Pages as one did in those days, I found out where it was and presented myself there one morning.

An elderly gent in tweed jacket and regimental tie asked me my business, very politely. I answered that I'd like to be an army officer and in particular one in a Scottish tank regiment. After a few pertinent questions he declared that '4 RTR are just the chaps for you!' and phoned up the regimental adjutant (I had no idea what an adjutant was at this point) and informed him that he had a potential officer candidate for him and that, with great enthusiasm, 'He's Scottish too!' I thought that was fairly self-evident, but let's just park that one for the moment.

Things then started to move quickly, because at the tender age of twenty-five I was, apparently, rather older than most who sought commissions in a front line tank regiment, and there was no time to lose. My first ever MoD Rail Warrant took me down to Regimental Headquarters of the Royal Tank Regiment (RHQ RTR), in those days in the rather splendid location of 1 Elverton Street, London SW1, where I met first the Regimental Adjutant (of whose job I was still completely ignorant) and then the Regimental Colonel, who somewhat confusingly held the rank of a major general.

Anyway, I must have passed muster because I was accepted as an officer candidate, subject to security clearances, medical, and passing the Regular Commissions Board (RCB) to get into RMAS. The medical threw up the first problem; I had a perforated eardrum, a relic of over enthusiastic diving in Govan Baths when I'd been learning to swim as a lad. I had to get it fixed, and quickly, otherwise they might not take me. There was too little time to join the NHS waiting list for the operation – known as a myringoplasty since you ask – so I went privately at the Victoria Infirmary in Glasgow. I seem to recall it cost me £420 in early 1980 (just short of £1,700 in 2021), which seemed an awful lot then and maybe it was, but I was dead keen.

That was the first hurdle out-of-the-way. My designated regiment, the 4th Royal Tank Regiment (Scotland's Own) (4 RTR or, more casually, 4th Tanks) to give it its proper title, was in Munster in what was then West Germany, and had planned to have me out for a visit. However, given the state of my lug, it was deemed a bit risky, so I got to visit one of the sister regiments, 3 RTR, on Salisbury Plain instead. The Third recruited in the West Country and were called the 'Armoured Farmers' by everyone else. They were very nice to me, and I remembered to hold my knife and fork correctly at dinner in the officers' mess. I also got my first ride in a Chieftain tank, which was a bit of an eye-opener. I was rather taken aback at just how big and heavy it was, and also how completely lacking in creature comforts it appeared to be, features which would become all too familiar in due course.

Chapter 2

After my visit to 3 RTR on Salisbury Plain, when I had my first hurl in a Chieftain tank, I was informed that I should proceed with my aspiration to join the regiment. I was, of course, pleased and relieved to have navigated the fast and tricky currents of regimental acceptance, but ahead lay the far choppier waters of the RCB and, *Insha'Allah*, the RMAS, the institution my dear old father had attended in 1946 and graduated from without too much difficulty, or so I assumed. It was now the sole centre for training officers for the British army, plus many overseas cadets as well.

The pressure was on. Like a fool I had told all my friends that 'I was going to Sandhurst' and then the awful reality of perhaps not being good enough to make it sunk in. The first big hurdle was RCB, but before that I attended something called pre-RCB as a taster for the real thing. I remember nothing about the pre-course except it took place at Catterick Camp in Yorkshire and we young hopefuls were collected from the station by the rudest and most unpleasant corporal it has ever been my misfortune to meet. Mind you, he was a Royal Hussar which goes a considerable way to explain it. More on the cavalry regiments of the British Army later!

RCB proper was held in those days in a wee town called Westbury, Wiltshire. Again, I have very little recollection of what happened during the three or so days I was there. I can remember giving a mini-lecture to my fellow aspirants on starting your own business, as I had whilst a university undergraduate to pay my way. There were also command tasks, leadership exercises in which each of us in turn were put in charge of the group and given a problem to solve. These were usually along the lines of 'you have to get that barrel across the minefield without it touching the ground using only the two staves and ball of string provided'. The briefing always ended with the question, 'How much time do you think you'll need?' Answer: 'Oh, about ten minutes'. Response: 'You've got four. Crack on!'

And there was an obstacle course to be negotiated, timed of course. It wasn't so much a test of strength or fitness but of nerve, courage, and confidence. There were always two ways of approaching each obstacle, one the safer and usually easier approach which took more time, and the other which was riskier, quicker, but carried more danger of failure. The only one I remember was the mock up of a house window; the option was either to use the conveniently placed plank to run up and lower yourself through the opening, or to tackle it some other way. I just had a hunch about this one and launched myself head first through the opening, to be greeted by a welcoming bed of soft sand on the other side. In doing so I caught my heel on the supporting scaffolding and brought the entire structure down. 'Do you want me to do it again?' I asked. I was told to 'crack on'. I had made the right choice.

We were also told that after the tests we could relax and there was no assessment in the evening in the officers' mess. Well, that was an outright fib and the sensible amongst us knew it.

Some of the young lads, however, took it at face value and drank the bar dry. I had a half of shandy and went early to bed. I wish I could say I then demolished a bottle of the Game Bird which I had secreted in my room but that wouldn't be true. I wasn't that savvy then.

And that was it. I passed. I still had no real idea what I was letting myself in for at this stage but all was going according to plan. Reality bit hard when I got to Sandhurst some months later. Lots of people I know loved being there, but for me it's six months of my life I'd rather forget. I guess that part of it was because most of my fellow officer cadets were straight out of university where many of them had been in the Officer Training Corps (OTC), whereas I'd come straight from two and a half years in a civilian job and was a bit older than most of them. Although I recognise it now, years later, I just thought that much of the regulation and discipline was just mindless BS. I also suspect that the initial impression I made on arrival was not so good, as I still sported my civvy longish hair. When I got it shorn in the first day the colour sergeant in charge ordered the rest of the squad to stop drilling, look, and laugh, which they did. That was OK though, because I knew I just looked like the rest of them then.

It was also exhausting. I wasn't fit enough when I turned up (how would I have known?) and the days were long and brutal. To add to my woes, after a few days at Sandhurst we deployed on exercise to a training area near Otterburn in the Scottish Borders. It was cold and wet and the first time I had been 'in the field' as they say, and the learning curve was very steep. The zip on my sleeping bag broke and I woke up frozen every night. My feet blistered in my new and as yet unbroken-in boots. This short exercise was primarily designed to root out those who didn't have the staying power for an army life, and shortly thereafter a few left the course.

Unfortunately for me, the combination of a badly blistered heel and wading through murky-water streams and burns resulted in an infected foot, which ballooned to the point where I could barely get my shoe on. On return to base I was packed off to the medical centre and prescribed a course of penicillin, administered of course by injections in the *bahookie*. I couldn't do much of the drill – square bashing – that was a staple of our daily existence, together with PT and various other robust activities that were the lot of an officer cadet.

The number of us who became *hors de combat* due to an ever-lengthening list of injuries grew exponentially, leading to some disquiet that some, although not all, were swinging the lead. Accordingly, at one morning parade, Captain Bob Stewart of the Cheshire Regiment who was one of our Directing Staff (DS), and who later in his military career was christened 'Bonking Bob from Bosnia' by the tabloids before going on to become a Conservative MP, addressed us. 'Officers', he said, 'do not go sick'. Sadly for him, this message was transmitted via a cadet patient to the senior medical officer in the academy, a fierce and belligerent Irishman of superior rank, who tore a strip off Cap'n Bob for such a stupid order. A quick reverse ferret ensued, and at a subsequent parade the order was rescinded.

Thankfully, we had some brilliant instructors, the non-commissioned officers (NCOs) I mean. Unlike many other militaries, the British Army's officer cadets are instructed mainly by NCOs, and the people selected to do this job are the best there are available. My platoon's NCO instructor was Colour Sergeant Brian Adams of the King's Own Scottish Borderers (KOSB) – you never forget these things – a smallish, hard little terrier of a man with a rare sense of humour and a hidden compassion and kindness for his charges. I'll never forget the swig he gave me from his hip flask when I was on a forced march and still a couple of miles out from the final destination and basically out on my feet. I made it.

Midway through the course, which I hated so much, I had decided that I wouldn't give up but would resign the day before the final parade, just to show them I'd won. This kept me going until the final exercise, which took place during a freezing March in Wales around the Brecon Beacons. The weather was foul, with snow and high winds, and by the end of it all my clothes and sleeping bag were soaking. It ended with a dawn attack on some enemy position, and we moved into the start line and lay down to wait for H-Hour. When the time came nothing happened; we had all fallen asleep in the snow and had to be woken up by the DS before the attack could proceed.

At the end of the course, having been spurred on latterly by the thought that my proposed dramatic resignation before the end would show them who was boss, I changed my mind. Inevitably, fitted out in my new uniform and with my parents and family down for the Pass Off Parade, what would have been a thoroughly futile gesture fell by the wayside. I was especially glad my Dad was in the stands when I got my commission. At the after party, he told me that the parade format and accompanying band music were exactly the same as at his parade in 1946. Some things never change.

Chapter 3

To preface what follows, I must just tell you that the regiment I joined after Sandhurst, the 4th Royal Tank Regiment (Scotland's Own), usually known as 4 RTR or 4th Tanks, was by common consensus the finest armoured regiment the world has ever seen. It was vastly superior to its cousins 1 RTR, 2 RTR, and 3 RTR, and was quite simply in a league of its own in the Royal Armoured Corps (RAC) in terms of style, panache, and sheer professionalism. No other armoured regiment has, or ever will, come close. Rommel's panzers don't even begin to compete. And please be assured there is no bias in my statement here, it is just plain fact, not opinion. Ask any of my former regimental comrades, whose contact details I can supply if required.

At this point it might be useful for the casual reader if I were to look in a little bit more detail at the history of the BARITWE (best armoured regiment in the world, ever). It started for 4 RTR, and indeed for the whole of the RTR, Royal Armoured Corps (RAC), and every other tank regiment worldwide in the First World War of 1914-18 when, as *any fule kno*, the tank was introduced by the British – with much encouragement from one Winston Churchill – as a means of breaking the deadlock of trench warfare on the Western Front.

Making its debut at Flers-Courcelette on the Somme on 15 September 1916, D Company of the Tank Corps, and later D Battalion, was the historical ancestor of 4th Tanks. Here the elementary mistake was made of 'penny-packeting' the tanks out in smaller numbers to support the attacking infantry and, whilst the presence of tanks came as a complete surprise to the enemy, their impact was not as great as had been hoped. Of the forty-nine available only eighteen had contributed to the battle, with many others broken down or bogged in the broken ground. Committing the few tanks that were available was seen at the time as having been a waste of the element of surprise that they had brought.

No such mistake was made at the Battle of Cambrai in November 1917. Here, a surprise attack used new tactics in a combined arms setting, involving nine battalions of the Tank Corps fielding 437 tanks between them in support of the infantry. The attack made rapid advances initially, but a combination of tank breakdowns and fierce German resistance limited this success, and the enemy regained much of the ground won via a series of energetic counterattacks. Nonetheless, this battle is regarded as the dawn of the age of the tank in warfare as we recognise it today, and placed the fledgling Tank Corps very much in the centre of the British army order of battle.

After peace came in 1918 the Tank Corps became the Royal Tank Corps (RTC), which in turn became the RTR just before the outbreak of war in 1939. There were actually three iterations of 4 RTR during the Second World War. The first was the regiment that deployed to France in 1939 as part of the BEF. Its most significant action was the Arras Counterattack on 21 May

1940, when in conjunction with its sister regiment 7 RTR and two battalions of the Durham Light Infantry (DLI) in support, it attacked Rommel's 7 Panzer Division and gave the Germans a bit of a fright, albeit at the loss of most of its tanks. This action may even have contributed to the decision by Mr Hitler to order his panzers to stop their dash for the Channel and helped get the remnants of the BEF away at Dunkirk, but we'll never really know. As it was, that was basically it for 4th Tanks. Most of those remaining got home in the evacuation but all its equipment was lost.

The second iteration which rose from the phoenix of the last (although 4 RTR didn't disappear altogether after Dunkirk) was reformed from the remnants of the regiment and 7 RTR, forming 4/7 RTR for a few months before returning to its proper title. After re-equipping and training in the UK it was sent to North Africa in 1941 to take Rommel and his panzers on again. Sadly, it was part of the Tobruk garrison which surrendered to the German/Italian enemy on 21 June 1942 and 'went into the bag' as the common parlance of the time might put it.

After that 4 RTR did not appear in the British army's order of battle until 1 March 1945 when, for reasons I don't fully understand 144 Regiment RAC was redesignated 4 RTR to replace the original immediately before the Rhine crossing Operation Plunder. 4 RTR crossed the Rhine in its Buffalo amphibious vehicles on the night of 23/24 March 1945, carrying infantry of the 5/7 Gordons and 5 Black Watch of the 51st (Highland) Division across the river. The regiment ended the war in northern Germany.

In the post war drawdown of the British army 4 RTR eventually amalgamated with 7 RTR but kept its title. After serving in various places around the rapidly diminishing British Empire, it saw out the majority of the rest of its days in Germany as part of the British Army of the Rhine (BAOR). Then, disastrously for all concerned, the BARITWE was amalgamated in 1993 with 1 RTR and was no more. Today there is only The Royal Tank Regiment, a single battalion sized tank outfit currently based in Tidworth on Salisbury Plan, where its predecessor 4 RTR had previously been stationed in 1982-84. This regiment carries on many of the traditions of the Fourth, including pipes and drums and the Hunting Rose tartan it wears, but is very definitely not the same.

When I joined 4 RTR in 1980 it was very firmly Scottish and called itself 'Scotland's Own'. I think we may have had the highest proportion of Scots soldiers in any of the Scottish regiments at that time, including the traditional infantry battalions of the Scottish Division, but I have no means of proving that claim. The association with Scotland had developed gradually over the regiment's history, and an important milestone had been the establishment of its pipes and drums, against general establishment disapproval and resistance, by Lieutenant Colonel Laurie New in the mid 1970s. Be that as it may, we recruited exclusively in Scotland by the time I joined, although a few from other parts of the UK and Commonwealth managed to sneak in. To use a football analogy, getting posted to 4 RTR was like being transferred to Real Madrid. Everybody who was anybody wanted to be part of it.

We weren't at all like our sister regiments, 1, 2, and 3 RTR, whom we regarded as nice enough but a bit pedestrian (although 1 RTR had an outstanding CO in Lieutenant Colonel Mark Goodson – but he was exported to them from 4 RTR to sort them out!). One senior retired general, who had all four RTR regiments in his command at one point or another, recently observed that '4 RTR was a Scottish regiment that just happened to share a cap badge with three others', and I think that's a fair summary of the situation. We didn't actually dislike the other RTR regiments, we just didn't seem to have very much in common with them. They were very fine regiments in their own right and had marvellous officers and soldiers. The fact that we felt we were different was hardly their fault, more perhaps the fault of RHQ RTR. That said, we always did feel that we were regarded as the black sheep of the family.

In many ways we probably had more in common with the cavalry, although you'd have to ask them about that as well. We called them 'donkey wallopers' and didn't really meet up with them in the field much, but there were friendships established on the various courses we attended together which last up to today. In Munster the 17/21st Lancers (17/21 L) were just down the road and there was much to-ing and fro-ing between the officers' messes at the time. They were a nice bunch and we had many friends there. I also got to know one or two officers from the Life Guards (LG), the Blues and Royals (RHG/D) and from other cavalry regiments and they always seemed pretty sound to me. Heaven forfend, but 4 RTR even ran the Tidworth Horse Trials one year! Our predecessors must have been turning in their graves, but it was actually great fun.

We did have a special affinity with the Royal Scots Dragoon Guards (Scots DG), much as we might refer to them as 'Scotland's other armoured regiment' when we wanted to irritate them. Their infamous officers' 'Long Range Destruction Group' was before my time, but its exploits during visits to our mess in Munster are the stuff of legend. During the 1991 Gulf War we supplied them with a handful of subalterns and other ranks who saw action with them during the ground war, all of whom were most complimentary about their wartime comrades when they returned. I knew a few of their officers fairly well as did others.

We were therefore hugely disappointed when we learned that, during the rationalisation of the RAC that followed the 1991 Gulf War, the RTR hierarchy spurned an approach from them suggesting that they might amalgamate with us, as seemed eminently sensible as we shared exactly the same recruiting area. That new regiment would have been a force to be reckoned with, and what a pipe band it would have had! Sadly, as previously noted, 4 and 1 RTR amalgamated in 1993 to form a new 1 RTR, and the Fighting Fourth disappeared from the British army's order of battle for good, much to everyone's regret.

Chapter 4

Having got that out of the way, I do have to tell you that my arrival at the BARITWE, then stationed at York Kaserne, Munster, Westphalia, was a tad underwhelming. For reasons that can be only properly explained by those involved at the time – I'm looking at you, adjutant and chief clerk (no names, no pack drill) – communications with those outwith the regiment's immediate geographic location were tenuous at best, and chaotic the rest of the time. That I was unable to get hold of my regimental accoutrements whilst I was at Sandhurst was just one instance of this.

So I more or less made my own way there, under my own steam as it were, armed only with an MoD posting order to guide me. I found myself on the regular RAF trooping flight from Luton to RAF Gutersloh, on which, to my chagrin and embarrassment, it was announced to the cabin full of rowdy soldiers returning from leave that 2nd Lieutenant Crawford was officer-in-charge of personnel in transit, an announcement greeted with a ribald cheer by my fellow passengers. As it happened my duties were nil, thank goodness.

Nobody met me at the airport – communications really were shambolic – so I got on the normal trooping bus heading for Munster, which was fine. I arrived at the entrance to York

Kaserne just as the guard was being mounted at 6.00 pm. Normally the mounting of the guard was a fairly formal affair, with the orderly officer of the day in full rig inspecting the guard with much saluting, crashing of feet, and swords being waved about. To my mild surprise I noted that the orderly officer that evening, one Lieutenant Steve Anstey, had decided not to bother with all the formal stuff, had driven the short distance from the officers' mess to the guardroom in his car, whereupon he wound down the window and said something along the lines of: 'Very good, Sergeant McDonald, fall them out and crack on.'

I introduced myself as the new officer joining the regiment. From the blank look on his face I could tell straight away that this was complete news to him. Nobody seemed to know I was coming out to Germany, and no room had been allocated to me in the officers' mess. But I got a bed for the night, in the orderly officer's bunk, something to eat (and no doubt something to drink as well – I can't remember) and all was well in the end. I had arrived.

The next morning I got into my uniform, had breakfast, and walked down to Regimental Headquarters (RHQ) for my welcome interview with the Commanding Officer (CO), Lieutenant Colonel Mike Rose, a delightful man, and was duly despatched to the D Squadron office as their new, wet-behind-the-ears, troop leader. The squadron was commanded by Major Mike Williams, I was told, and at the designated time I marched into his office, gave him my best Sandhurst crashing-to-attention salute, and said something like: '2nd Lieutenant Crawford reporting for duty, Sir!' Mike looked up from his desk somewhat bemusedly, and kindly informed me that we didn't go in for that sort of nonsense in the Fourth and that I should call him Mike from then on. I learned that all officers in the regiment were to be addressed by their first names regardless of rank and seniority. The exception was the CO, who was addressed as 'Colonel' or, if you were feeling relaxed, confident, or slightly tipsy, you might occasionally address him as 'Colonel Mike'.

By far and away the most terrifying part, though, was meeting the troops you were to command for the first time. This took place the next morning after my arrival at first parade, a short little ceremony held on the tank park at 8.00 am each working day. I was to take over 13 Troop, D Squadron, from Richard 'Stig' Jenkinson. I knew the boys were eyeing me up just as I was them. It was all a bit discombobulating, to be honest, but I survived. I think I was tested by the troop in my first couple of days because when I asked if I could help on the tank park I was given the task of crawling underneath one of the panzers and hammering away at something by my first troop sergeant, Jimmy Mullen. From my prone position when so engaged I noticed a large number of pairs of boots coming to the tank to observe the new officer at work. And after about fifteen minutes I was told that was good enough. I don't think it helped with the maintenance one iota!

The relationship with your first command, your first troop, was an interesting one. They desperately wanted you to be good, and you desperately wanted them to like you. Some young officers had just got it and succeeded instantaneously, gaining both the respect and liking of their men (it was all men in my day). Others never had it and fell by the wayside ere too long, back to civvy street after their three years and, it has to be said, some of them to do great things and achieve high office. But even if your boys thought you were a complete muppet, as long as you were an honest, decent, well-intentioned-trying-your-best muppet, then eventually you became *their* muppet. They'd still call you a muppet amongst themselves, but if anyone from outside voiced the same opinion about *their* officer they'd get battered, simple as. I would never condone such violence, of course, but I'm sure there's a lesson there somewhere for the corporate world.

Chapter 5

What follows is an attempt to describe what it was like being a young-ish, single, junior officer in a Germany-based Scottish armoured regiment in the 1980s. I hardly know where to begin to be honest, there is so much to cover. I have also had to be cautious with the detail in some of the anecdotes; many of the better ones could possibly lead to separations, divorces, or indeed defamation actions in the courts, so I have omitted some of the very best stories – for now, anyway.

Perhaps the best place to start is with a brief description of 4 RTR's barracks at the time of my joining, York Kaserne, in Munster. Briefly, they dated back to the 1930s and had, we were led to believe, been occupied by a Luftwaffe flak battalion during the Second World War. There was no sign of their previous occupation, no statues, regalia, swastikas or the like, but the buildings were recognisably Teutonic, solid, brick built and with extensive cellars. The base was arranged around a parade square with a rectangular road round it, on either side of which were the buildings occupied by our personnel and vehicles.

Of particular relevance to my account here were two buildings which were sited in one corner of the set up near the main gate, namely the officers' mess and the officers' mess annex, separated by a single tennis court and a bit of garden. The mess building held the dining room, anterooms, bar, a couple (I think) of bedrooms upstairs for senior single officers, and a cellar wherein the billiard table lurked. Together with terrace, garden with ornamental pond, and pleasant entrance hall it was in pretty good order. We used to sit out on the terrace a lot in the good weather, and entertain guests there too. Occasionally the croquet enthusiasts would get out in the garden for a few matches, which could become highly competitive between subalterns.

In contrast, the mess annex was a shambles, a chaotic jumble of subalterns' rooms on two floors, assorted bits of cars and motorbikes, and the occasional girlfriend threading her way along the corridors through the broken beer bottles. This is where all the real action took place, of which more later. Very occasionally an overly zealous CO would announce his intention to inspect, and there would be a flurry of activity as said motorbikes, car parts, girlfriends and broken bottles were removed, but for most of the time it was reminiscent of a battlefield. Nowadays the environmental health police would close it down. It was a bit of a dive if we're being honest.

Everyday life for a junior officer at that time consisted of about ten per cent 'work', seventy per cent idleness, and ten per cent hedonistic mayhem, proportions which could shift significantly from time to time, usually to the benefit of the mayhem. A normal working day would start with breakfast in the mess, individually cooked to order and brought to the table by the mess waiter, followed by first parade at 8.00 am, when you met up with your troop on the tank park and discussed the day's business. The tank park was the preserve of your troop sergeant, and he didn't want any young officer hanging around for too long distracting the boys from their work, so we usually took the hint and disappeared after about ten minutes or so. During the handover of the troop from the wonderful Stig Jenkinson to me, I asked him what I should do now that first parade was over. He replied, 'If I were you I'd just go back to bed'. I have never forgotten his sound advice.

Next came coffee break at 10.00 am, held in the officers' coffee room in the RHQ block. Many young officers avoided this altogether, for it was a perfect opportunity for you to be 'bubbled' (ie nominated for some unwelcome task) by the adjutant who would seek out the unsuspecting there. Thereafter there were two long hours to fill before lunch, again held in the mess and at which it was not unheard of to consume four or five beers in preparation for the rigours of the afternoon. Perhaps unsurprisingly, there was much sneaking back to your room for a nap before afternoon tea was served at 4.30 pm or thereabouts, at which more beers might be consumed as well as tea and toast. There then followed another long three hours before dinner, a formal event for which we dressed in suits during the week and jackets and ties at the weekend. In exceptionally hot weather we might adopt 'planter's order', in which jackets were dispensed with but shirt sleeves remained firmly rolled down and ties were properly worn.

Dinner could be great fun or tedious, depending mainly on the personality of the senior officer present, who presided. If he was a good guy it was great fun, if he was a bore or a bully, or sometimes both, it wasn't such good fun. In either case, Herculean amounts of alcohol were consumed. Then we went to bed, eventually, and repeated the whole process the next day. With the benefit of hindsight I think we were all teetering on the edge of alcoholism, but we were young and foolish and it was all one big laugh.

As you may have surmised, there were huge amounts of downtime, and those hours were filled by a variety of pursuits. Some played lots of sport, tennis, rugby and squash mainly. 4 RTR had a historical tradition with motorbikes, and there were always two or three parked outside, and oftentimes inside, the annex in varying states of repair and reassembly. We weren't hugely into cars except when torching them, of which more later. The more intellectually minded officers, always viewed with a bit of suspicion, wrote and painted, and some played musical instruments. I had my guitar, which some saw as decidedly dodgy and a sure sign that the regiment was going to the dogs.

There was also much going downtown to the various bars and tearooms that Munster had to offer. The Germans do *kaffee und kuchen* extremely well, right up there with their skills at building cars and invading neighbouring countries. The local German population was kind and friendly to us as a rule, although I sometimes wondered whether our black uniforms and berets might remind them of unhappier times. As there was a big student population, we also thought that it might give us an opportunity to chat up the pretty female students we saw everywhere, but the military was not popular amongst them and most attempts crashed and burned before we even got to the flak and searchlights, if you know what I mean. *Wie schade*!

Occasionally you would be orderly officer for the day, or sometimes for the week, fortnight, or even month if you had transgressed excessively. It was hardly an onerous duty, but necessitated being in uniform all day – service dress up until 6.00 pm then patrol blues thereafter – and carrying out various duties at the behest of the adjutant. Armouries were inspected and weapons counted, soldiers under sentence (ie in the guardroom for some misdemeanour) were visited ('No requests or complaints, Sir!') and food sampled at the boys' mealtimes in the cookhouse. The soldiers' breakfast was a particular favourite of mine as it allowed me to sample the sausages on offer; we didn't get them in the mess as they were rather haughtily deemed 'not officer food'. Finally, and as previously noted, you would mount the guard at the guardroom at 6.00 pm and visit them during the wee small hours, the timing of which was decided by the roll of a dice on the adjutant's desk when you reported for duty that morning. I always stuck rigorously to the time allocated to me and appeared at the guardroom in full patrol blues, no matter how unearthly the hour. Others smarter than me strolled over there just before bed time in their civvies and, in cahoots with the guard commander, came to an agreement on the time that their visit would be recorded in the log book.

And that just about sums up the ten per cent work and seventy per cent idleness that was the lot of a young officer in barracks. I shall now endeavour to do justice to the remaining ten percent of hedonistic madness, which was the best part of all. It's hard to explain why and when things sometimes just exploded, often literally. It could happen because it was someone's birthday, or somebody was being posted away or leaving altogether, or sometimes just because the stars aligned and it was that time. To put it into context, we were young, single, fit and trained for something we all hoped would never happen, that is confronting the vast Soviet tank armies just across the border in East Germany. We were also far from home with time on our hands. To paraphrase another time, we were overpaid, oversexed, and over there.

When all sense of decorum broke down the resultant behaviour could be outrageous, inexcusably destructive, and sometimes downright dangerous. On the plus side, most of the times were, and are even more so with hindsight, excruciatingly funny. Oh how we laughed. Things usually started to go astray at dinner. We had a privileged and luxurious lifestyle in the mess, and by virtue of being overseas we were paid a local overseas allowance (LOA) on top of our salaries. In addition to this we had a certain tax-free status – a carton of 200 Benson & Hedges cigarettes cost £2, and a bottle of Taittinger champagne, our favourite at the time, could be had for less than £12 a bottle at one point. I remember quite clearly a night when there were twenty-five young officers at dinner, and each of us had a bottle of Taittinger in front of us. When we ran out of champagne a four tonne truck was despatched with driver and the mess steward to Reims across the border in France to get some more. Happy days indeed.

An early sign of matters going further awry might be the sight of officers returning to the annex carrying crates of beer. The 4 RTR officers' mess beer of choice was Carlsberg *hof*, not the sort of rubbish in cans that you get in the UK these days, but the real McCoy, in small bottles, from the Carlsberg brewery in Denmark (accept no substitute would be my advice). The empty bottles lent themselves to a number of pastimes. The most innocuous of these would be Carlsberg skittles, wherein the lower corridor of the annex would constitute the bowling alley, the bottles were the skittles, and the balls were usually croquet balls liberated from the croquet lawn. It was great fun, if a little noisy and destructive (of the bottles). I liked to think of it as recreational recycling, and it was very therapeutic.

More entertaining by far was the game known as 'Jeux Sans Frontieres Carlsberg'. Most of our bedrooms had two or three windows, and the format was this; after a few of the Carlsberg bottles had been emptied via the usual means, each person present was in turn blindfolded and handed an empty bottle. One of the windows was then opened fully whilst the others remained closed. The player was then spun around several times whilst still blindfolded and then had to throw the bottle where he best calculated the open window would be, with fairly predictable results. It's a great game, and may be entirely appropriately adopted across the UK at times of lockdown or other government-imposed *diktats*. Fun for all the family.

Pyrotechnics also played a large part in our after dinner and weekend antics. When in the field on exercise with our tanks we were liberally supplied with various pyrotechnics to add realism to the training. We were meant to hand all the unused ones back to the Regimental Quartermaster Sergeant (RQMS) at the end of the training period, but of course we never did. The annex therefore became a veritable arsenal of military grade pyrotechnic devices just waiting to be put to alternative recreational use.

Three devices in particular were especially popular: the smoke grenade, the thunderflash, and the Schermuly. Smoke grenades were jam jar sized devices where you unscrewed the top and then yanked it firmly, whereupon brightly coloured smoke gushed in abandon. They were useful for smoking out friends who were being 'boring' by hiding in their rooms behind locked doors, or entertaining 'guests'. Knock a quick hole in the skylight above the door, pop in a couple of smoke grenades, and after twenty seconds or so the door would open and half clothed guests would scurry away down the corridor, their hair and bodies dyed deep red and orange from the smoke. Or, more subtly, tie the grenade to the underside of a friend's car, unscrew the top and then tie it to some unmoveable object. The victim would then be followed by a plume of smoke billowing out behind when they next drove their car. Top bantz!

Thunderflashes produced a loud bang and puff of white smoke, ideal for waking up those who chose to sleep in late or more generally for enhancing any sort of party. They came with a five to seven second delay once the fuse was lit, and were pretty loud – 119 dB at twelve metres (whatever that means) – particularly within the confines of a room. They also had the added benefit of occasionally blowing out the windows, an early form of air conditioning much in evidence in the annex.

The Schermuly, on the other hand, was a 'single use disposable parachute flare that produced a 80,000 candle power light (ie pretty bright) that burned for about thirty seconds at a height of 300 metres' if launched vertically. Ideal for lighting up the scene, and enhancing the mood, at any party when it got a bit dark. Better than that, however, was that some genius had worked out that you could tape three thunderflashes to a Schermuly, light their fuses, then launch the flare into the Heavens where it would go off with a humungous bang at about 1,000 feet, rattling the windows for miles around. It was like being in an air raid, as those of us who experienced the SCUD rocket attacks in Riyadh in 1991 will know, but I'm getting a bit ahead of myself here.

I could go on for ever. You could be woken from your slumbers by an officer on his trail bike (actually, it was Nick Horne, no denying it I'm afraid) entering your room, riding it over your bed, with you and anyone else who happened to be in it at the time for that matter, and then leaving again whence he had come, not a word being spoken. It wasn't mentioned again, just as if it had never happened. Or you, your bed and mattress, with you in it, could be hoisted out of the window just for fun at any time of the day or night. Thankfully this latter activity was confined to those on the ground floor, which made a top floor room very attractive.

I mentioned cars previously, saying that we weren't particularly into them except as bonfire fuel. 'Torching' a car didn't happen that often, but when it did it usually involved the vehicle of some brother officer who was away on leave or on a course somewhere. These 'car-b-cues' usually involved old bangers, but you had to be careful what you were doing; more than once others' newer cars were blistered by the resultant infernos, including the senior member's Porsche. Most famous of all, and just before my time to be honest, was the occasion when the brigadier's wife, after a formal function at which her husband and she were the senior guests, commandeered the old mess banger, drove it round and round the garden, and finally deposited it in the ornamental pond. And then threw a lighted match in the petrol tank. Good game, good game!

Getting cooler on the mess veranda as the sun begins to set? No problem, just pile up the garden furniture and set it alight to keep you warm. To be fair, this was one occasion the Quartermaster (QM) and the CO didn't see the funny side, and there was a bit of a downer on those involved thereafter, so I'm told. Not that it excuses any of the destructive behaviour, but the damage was always paid for by the perpetrators, sometimes with a 'voluntary donation' to the RTR Benevolent Fund on top.

We did enjoy rather more formal affairs as well, usually commemorating one of the 4 RTR battle honours. In order of the annual calendar they were as follows. First, on or around 23 March, was Rhine Crossing, which celebrated 4 RTR's participation in Op Plunder in 1945. During that operation the regiment, commanded by Lieutenant Colonel Alan Jolly DSO, had carried the infantry of the 51st Highland Division across the river in their Buffalo tracked amphibious vehicles. This commemoration was very much an officers' mess event, and usually took the form of a formal mess dinner with guests, at the end of which a large piece of silverware called the Bull's Head Cup was filled with champagne and passed round the table several times for all to drink from, at the end of which it was replenished and presented to the junior subaltern by the CO to finish off and upend the empty Cup on his head, sometimes standing on the table. Fittingly, the Cup was made from the melted down silver of the 79th Armoured Division, under whose command the regiment had been on the day.

Next up was another officers' mess event, the Arras Ball, held on or around 21 May to commemorate the action in 1940 when 4 and 7 RTR thrust into Rommel's 7 Panzer Division and arguably contributed to the delay that let much of the British Expeditionary Force (BEF) escape from Dunkirk in the following days. This was the major event of the year and was always long in the planning. We also paid for it by a levy on our mess bills all year round. It was a proper ball, with a formal meal followed by dancing and other activities like roulette and blackjack and went on into the early hours. Girlfriends and significant others usually came out from the UK when we were in Germany and were put up at the local hotels or by married officers in their married quarters (MQs). As befitted such a formal event behaviour tended to be much more subdued.

The third major event on the regimental calendar was Cambrai Day, always pronounced by the boys as 'Cambria' for reasons I've never understood. This commemorated the first use of massed tank attack by the British at Cambrai in France in 1917. This was very much an all ranks affair, and started by the officers serving the soldiers 'gunfire', essentially tea with a stiff measure of rum in it, as had been done before H-Hour in 1917. This led into a fairly boisterous day of events including sports and formal dinners and balls in the various messes. The officers were always invited to the WOs and Sergeants' Mess as guests at their Cambrai Ball.

Talking of girlfriends as we were earlier, my comrades and I were not exactly starved of female company. Those invited to the Arras Ball tended to be 'serious' girlfriends, normally from London or occasionally other cities of the UK. Their visits could be regular in some cases but tended to be fleeting, leaving us wallowing in our usual all-male environment. The vacuum left was filled by other ex-pat Brits; the Queen Alexandra's Royal Army Nursing Corps (QARANC) nurses who staffed the British Military Hospital (BMH) Munster were frequent visitors to our mess, and some romances here blossomed into marriage.

Less favoured were the female member of the British Families Education Service (BFES), the teachers who educated the children of British servicemen and women in various garrisons in Germany and elsewhere. They were always referred to as 'the Screechers' which was less than complimentary and some were afforded nicknames according to their perceived pulchritude. Three I remember were named 'The Kamikaze Pilot', 'Helen The One-Eyed Frog', and 'The Iguana'. I never knew to whom these nicknames applied but they did make me laugh.

Very rarely one or two of us might have German girlfriends but it was fairly unusual. Despite the fact that Munster, for example, had a large student population, they tended to be quite vocally anti-military and treated we officers like lepers most of the time. The boys, on the other hand, had much better relationships with the local German girls and many of them married into German families with some remaining in Germany to this day, totally assimilated into the local communities.

However, I wouldn't want the casual reader to think that Britain's defences on the Iron Curtain were in any sort of jeopardy during such jolly times, or that we young officers of the BARITWE were dissolute, pampered and privileged rakes. Far from it, I think, but it's all a bit hazy to be honest. But in 4th Tanks, to paraphrase George Harrison, if you can remember Munster you weren't really there.

Chapter 6

Now I turn at long last to tanks and what it was like being a tank soldier in the last two decades of the twentieth century. Tank soldiers – the Americans call us 'tankers' which is an ugly word and another example of the creeping Americanisation of British culture which must be resisted at all costs – are a breed apart. If you have never commanded tanks or been part of a tank crew then you'll never fully understand. A bit like seeing Hendrix at Woodstock, if I can use a musical analogy. But I'll try to explain a little of what it was like.

First of all the vehicles. When I joined 4 RTR the Regiment was equipped with Chieftain Main Battle Tanks (MBT), mainly Mk3s and Mk5s if I can recall correctly. D Squadron had 14 of these, with four troops of three and squadron headquarters (SHQ) with two. My troop, 13 Troop, consisted of three Chieftains and twelve crewmen including myself, four crewmen to each tank. A tank crew consisted of a driver, gunner, loader/radio operator and commander.

All our tanks, and indeed all the supporting armoured vehicles in the regiment, carried 'Chinese Eyes' painted on the turret or on the side of the hull. Now, there is some controversy in RTR circles as to exactly how the eyes came to be associated with 4th Tanks, but the version in the official histories is as follows. In 1918 the Chinese member of the Federal Council of Malaya presented the British government with a Mark V tank. In accordance with the Chinese practice of painting eyes on their boats and junks, he stipulated that the tank should carry them also, with the rational that, 'No got eyes, how can see? No can see, how can savee? No can savee, how can chop chop?' The gifted tank was issued to D Battalion of the RTC, and 4 RTR, as the descendant of that battalion, carried on the tradition.

Similarly, all tanks and armoured vehicles were named. The original tanks of D Company of the Heavy Branch Machine Gun Corps (HBMGC), the historical antecedent of both the RTC and RTR, were all named with words beginning with the letter D. This was formalised when the 4th Battalion of the RTC adopted the practice with the following scheme: A Squadron names began with 'Da', B Squadron with 'De', C Squadron with 'Di', and RHQ with 'Do' and 'Du'. Later, when D Squadron was reconstituted as a tank squadron it used a variety of different names beginning with 'D'. The exception was OC B Squadron's tank which was renamed *Royal Sovereign* after Her Majesty The Queen visited 7 RTR in Catterick in 1957 and 4 RTR inherited the name on amalgamation. My first tank was named *Dalmellington* after the village in Ayrshire.

Now to the panzers themselves. The Chieftain has a bit of a chequered history and reputation. Designed as the replacement for Britain's highly successful post war Centurion, it never quite achieved the fine reputation of its predecessor. In many ways it might have been too innovative too soon. Great effort went into lowering the silhouette of the tank whilst protecting it with the thickest armour, and to that end the driver drove in a supine position (when closed down) on a reclining seat, looking through a periscope sight. The armour was pretty thick too, presenting roughly fifteen and a half inches of armour to horizontal attack in the frontal arc.

The 120 mm rifled gun was pretty good for the time too. It was innovative in that, rather than using fixed ammunition which necessitated the storage or ejection of spent shell cases, it went down the naval route of having separate rounds and propellant charges. This allowed the propellant – the 'bag charges' – to be stowed below the turret ring in pressurised 'wet' containers which would, in theory, prevent combustion should the tank be penetrated by hostile fire. The penalty was, of course, that loading two-piece ammunition, plus the cartridge that fired the whole sheboodle off, took slightly longer than conventional one piece ammo. But the gun itself was accurate and we had every confidence in it.

What let Chieftain down was the engine, which was forever breaking down. In fact, it was a common saying that Chieftain was the best tank in the world as long as it broke down in a good firing position. Sadly, unreliability of automotive aspects is a recurring theme in the history of British tank design stretching back to before the Second World War. The basic problem seemed to be that the Chieftain engine was originally designed to be multi-fuel, an over-complication, and originally produced only 650 bhp for a fifty-six tonnes tank, so it was chronically underpowered as well. For comparison, modern tanks have engines producing up to 1500 bhp or more.

This unreliability made us – or more accurately the boys – slaves to our tanks, forever working on them, repairing them, maintaining them. How we envied the Germans with their Leopard 1s, who parked them up on a Friday, went home for the weekend, then started them up on Monday morning and off they went. Yes, they might have had thinner armour and a less powerful gun, but at least they could *rely* on them to work, and they weren't half fast as well.

But, while I don't think we ever came to love our Chieftains, we did sort of like them. Sure, they were demanding masters, but when you got them to work as designed they were sweet to be in. Unlike the young men of the RAC nowadays, we got to take our tanks out a lot on exercise, or 'scheme' as the boys called it. A troop leader could still decide to take his troop out to the local training area if he could persuade the squadron leader it was a good idea, for example, even though it would involve the Royal Military Police (RMP) and German *Polizei* stopping the traffic as the tanks exited the barracks and headed out on the civilian roads.

That said, it must have been a complete pain in the backside for the local German population. Our local training area in Munster was a pocket-handkerchief sized training area know as the Dorbaum, which we used for low level training or as our 'crash out' location when exercising our deployment plans at short notice, usually when Exercise Active Edge was called. Active Edge could be called at any level, from the CO wanting to test his regiment right up to 1st British Corps (1 BR Corps) crashing out more or less all the British troops in Germany. It could happen at any time of the day or night, and it was not unknown for mess dinner nights to be ended abruptly by it, with some officers deploying still dressed in their formal mess kit.

To get to the Dorbaum we had to use the local roads, and many an incident occurred. Occasionally a tank would throw off a rubber track pad from its track, a heavy piece of material, which might bounce off the road and through the windscreen of a civilian car following. This could, and did sadly, result in serious injury. Or a tank might dump all its engine oil on the highway, turning it into a skidpan with obvious results for local traffic. On one occasion one of our Chieftain's brakes failed at the junction where we turned to head for the training areas and it ploughed straight on, taking all the traffic lights out in its path although, thankfully, avoiding civilian casualties. And, on a more personal note, I once drove back to barracks with my troop at rush hour, and the only way I could get past the traffic was by going up on the newly made pavement, ripping up the paving stones, much to the annoyance of the German workers who had laid them minutes beforehand. It was either that or bring Munster to a halt – what else could I do?

Larger scale manoeuvre training was usually carried out on the Soltau Training Area (SLTA) up on the Luneberg Heath and close to where Monty had accepted the German partial surrender on 8 May 1945. The old maps show its extent – the red areas being for tank movement if you have access to one – and most of 1 (Br) Corps had become familiar with it over the past forty years or so before I first set foot, or more accurately track, on it. The old hands had been there so many times they didn't even need the map to navigate it, but to a new boy it could be difficult, especially at night. On my first night march test as troop leader I got hopelessly lost, managed to check in at about three of the ten rendezvous points laid out for us, and eventually waited until dawn broke to get my bearings. Hardly an auspicious start, but I was to learn I wasn't the first or last to experience such a debacle.

All those years of tracked movement over a relatively small area had rendered the soil into a fine sand-like dust, and by the laws of physics (which I was taught but have forgotten) the open spaces were configured like waves in the open sea, so that driving your tank across was a constant rearing and diving motion which occasionally made people seasick. The sparsely wooded areas were where we bivvied up at night and slept on the back decks under tank sheets, not a particularly pleasant experience in retrospect but at the time we hardly noticed. Once one of our support four-tonner lorries caught fire and burned out, but the CO just borrowed a JCB from the sappers, dug a big hole, and dumped the remains in it before covering over. It's probably still there, waiting to be unearthed by some archaeologist of the future. We weren't particularly eco-conscious in those days I'm afraid.

It's high time I talked about the boys. Other Scottish regiments might have called them the Jocks, but to us in the 4 RTR officers' mess they were always 'the boys'. And they still are, even though we're all in our sixties and seventies, and I suspect it will ever be thus. They were, and are, a splendid bunch, not perfect (who is?) but generally hard-working, professional, and endlessly amusing. They were tough too, not in any thuggish way, but in a non-complaining manner regardless of how tired, cold or hungry they might have been.

Most hailed from the Glasgow area or Fife, it seemed, with a smattering of wild men from the Highlands and islands. I am not much given to sentimentality, but I'm so pleased I had the opportunity to get to know all of them.

Being on tanks was a rough life. Aside from the constant maintenance and repair of the unreliable Chieftain, the noise and vibration could be exhausting. On exercise we were filthy despite washing and shaving every morning. Such was the dust thrown up by the tracks and oil from the engine our faces often matched the black denims we wore, and days after returning to camp we still had 'panda eyes' from the ingrained dirt around our peepers. We couldn't change our clothes much, nor bathe except for the rare run into camp in the truck for a shower if we were lucky. Famously one of my fellow officers, who was married, would be provided with a clean pair of underpants by his wife for every day he was on scheme. He would wear one pair throughout and then stamp the rest in the dirt and dust before returning home to show his wife that he had, indeed, changed them often!

On the other hand, if you haven't experienced bouncing over the countryside in a well crewed tank with the wind in your hair, and probably a fag in your mouth, then you haven't really lived. As Samuel Johnson said, 'Every man thinks meanly of himself for not having been a soldier', but that was before tanks were invented. Otherwise he would have been more specific and added 'tank' before 'soldier'!

I don't think you ever forget your first tank crew. Although it did change from time to time because of leave, courses, and postings, the classic crew of my tank call-sign T41 during my lamentably short spell as a troop leader was: driver, Bob Withington (addressed as 'Dick' for obvious reasons); gunner, George Gillespie; and loader, Eck McKenzie. The other two tanks in the troop were commanded by Sergeant Sneck McBride and Corporal John Barnwell. Together we managed our way through one complete training season comprising dry training (ie no live ammunition) at SLTA, gunnery training at Hohne ranges, and then the full *bhuna* – manoeuvre and live firing in Alberta, Canada. I will write more about the latter two events in due course.

The basic building blocks of it all were the low-level troop training drills and exercises which we carried out first, followed by squadron and then regimental, or battle group (BG) training which upped the ante a bit. Up and down and across Soltau we went, practising advances to contact, quick attacks, defensive tactics and that most difficult skill of all, the withdrawal in contact. At night we moved into hides in the woods, replenned and maintained the panzers. If we were lucky we got a moment to relax over a beer or two. We always had alcohol on our tanks. A standard load if there were such a thing might be two slabs (one slab equals twenty-four cans) of Tennents or McEwans on the turret floor and a bottle of The Famous Grouse whisky in the turret bin. Infantry regiments who saw our boys drinking on scheme were aghast, but for us it was normal.

In the late summer/early autumn, when the German farmers had harvested their crops, there might be a field training exercise (FTX), when we practised our trade in normal countryside, driving up roads and through fields, and sometimes walls and fences, just like we thought we would in reality. These were usually held at divisional level – there were four divisions in 1 (Br) Corps at the time – but sometimes the whole corps would turn out, and the 'enemy' would be played by the Americans or the Germans. These were on a different scale altogether and I'll be writing about one of them in particular in a later chapter. In all of them we were followed around by Damage Control (DAMCON) parties who sorted out compensation for the damage that we caused. Sometimes the German farmers would stop us and ask us to knock down a particular wall or barn that needed replacing, and on at least one such FTX the exercise had to stop because we ran out of compensation money. Happy days.

Tanks were an 'elf 'n' safety nightmare, mind, notwithstanding the designers' attempts to incorporate numerous safety devices. You couldn't fire the gun, for example, without the loader's guard being pulled back into position which shielded him from the recoil. But if you were on dry training and going cross country at night, and if your loader was standing behind the breech making a brew in the boiling vessel (BV – one of the few things American 'tankers' envied us for was our BVs, which meant we could conjure up hot food and drinks without stopping) and you hit a tree or other obstruction with the gun barrel, it could recoil and break his pelvis, as happened on at least one occasion. Or if your gunner fell asleep and the commander traversed the turret his ankle could be broken if his feet were in the wrong position. I dropped the lid on my cupola on my head more than once, and people were forever jamming fingers in various places. Not for nothing did every tank commander carry four syrettes of morphine round his neck on scheme.

Saddest of all, on one or two occasions we lost one of the boys, usually when a tank tipped over. The drill if that happened was, counter intuitively, to drop inside the turret; the natural instinct was to try and jump out, and if you did that you'd get squished. Not nice.

The highlight of being out on exercise, though, was undoubtedly the squadron smoker, particularly on Soltau. The German civilian authorities had imposed a ban on all tracked movement on the area over the weekend, quite understandably in retrospect because of the noise, dust and smoke, so all tank movement stopped and we moved into hides in the woods for rest and maintenance. We could get the shower truck into Rheinsehlen Camp for a cleanup, and then, on Saturday night, came the great event. The Squadron Quartermaster Sergeant (SQMS) would arrive with the normal evening replen of rations and fuel, and also an ample supply of beer for the boys to purchase. It seemed that one slab – twenty-four cans – per person was deemed appropriate.

Meanwhile, those spared guard and maintenance tasks had been collecting a vast pile of firewood, maybe not rivalling the Shankhill Road bonfires on the twelfth of July but a good attempt. After work was done, and after the evening meal, the squadron would congregate around the vast pile, sitting on the slabs of beer they had bought, and the fire would be lit with the help of much oil ('mair lube, mair lube') from the tanks. They usually went up with a 'whoosh' and then the fun would begin. As the boys drank their beers, upon which they were sitting of course, their perches would become more and more unstable until they fell off their seats. All the while the fire was being fuelled by ever more branches and logs from the surrounding area until there was a danger that the whole wood would go on fire and burn all our tanks and equipment with it. Thankfully this never happened, not in my experience anyway.

As the evening wore on there would be some good natured banter, usually about burning the Catholics in the assembled company, especially the Catholic officers, and then at some point the dreaded cry of 'jump the fy-err!' would be heard, at which point all sensible officers would quickly retire. Jumping the *fy-err* involved taking a running jump over the hopefully slightly diminished fire and landing safely on the other side. All the better if you did it stark, bollock naked. Quite a few of the young bloods didn't quite make it and got singed landing short. One of our more spirited young officers, whom everyone called, and still calls, 'The Wean' because of his relative youth (shall I name him? Oh, OK I will; it was Niall Macnaughton) and who had decided to stay the course, managed the feat in his birthday suit. Sadly no photographs exist of his triumph.

He does recall, though, that on landing on the far side of the *fy-err* he was hosed down with beer by his troop and rolled in the sandy soil by them as a reward for his valour. He described to me, just the other day, waking up naked in his sleeping bag and, holding it round his waist, hopping round the assorted recumbent bodies that had fallen asleep around the embers of the fire whilst he recovered his clothes. The scene would resemble the fall of Stalingrad, with some individuals literally smouldering in their slumbers having stayed too close to the embers. On another famous occasion, upon return to barracks, one senior NCO's wife marched into her husband's squadron leader's office and gave him a piece of her mind about the state in which her spouse had returned from one such event, badly singed as he was.

These were great times, and like all great times you only realise how great they were when they're gone. Today's army, I understand, would not tolerate similar behaviour and is altogether more serious and disciplined about its calling. More's the pity in many ways, and I would still bet they aren't as good as we were.

Chapter 7

And so to ranges, or firing camp as some other regiments called it. This happened once every year or two years depending on which particular training cycle you found yourself on. We took it very seriously, as all good regiments did, because unlike manoeuvre training where your performance could rest on the opinion of the senior officer present, on the ranges your performance was easily measurable by the number of holes you put in the target and the time it took you to do it. So we were on our mettle and, for those horrified by the bacchanalian excesses recounted in the last chapter, there was nigh on no alcohol either, during working hours at least.

Training started in camp on various training aids which simulated the real thing. My first year I hadn't completed my troop leader's course before I joined the regiment and so, quite rightly, wasn't entrusted to command a tank at ranges. However it was thought a good idea that I should be the squadron 2ic's (second-in-command's) loader during firing, which was good experience before going off to Lulworth in Dorset where RAC gunnery training takes place. Initial loaders' training took place in a simulator (SIM), a sort of open plan, tank turret mock-up with a pretty faithful working reproduction of the gun breech crew stations, and ammunition stowage.

Of course the practice ammunition was inert, which is just as well because in my very first attempt at the loader's drill I dropped the round – I hadn't expected it to be so heavy! As the only officer in my class of about eight there was much smirking and tittering from the rest, but it was much warranted. I didn't drop one again. Meanwhile the commanders and gunners went through their own simulator the name of which I have forgotten but ended up with airgun pellets being fired at rubber tank targets in a sand box on a miniature range. Sophisticated it wasn't, and I guess it must have been of Second World War vintage at least.

Anyway, after a few weeks' build up we would then embark en masse for Hohne Ranges just up the road, tanks and drivers by rail or transporter and rest by road. Nowadays I understand that, under some scheme called Whole Fleet Management (WFM), you only have a few tanks for training in barracks and the rest you sign out like hire cars for field training and ranges. None of that back in the day, we owned our own tanks and took them with us (Canada excepted) for training.

The loading up of our tanks in barracks if we were going by road brought a little bit of post war history with it. One of the tank transporter regiments was formed by the 'Mojos', members of the BAOR's Mixed Service Organisation (MSO) comprising former PoWs and Displaced Persons (DPs) who either couldn't or wouldn't return home at the end of the war. Many of them were Poles who did not wish to return to their home country whilst it was under communist rule.

In any case, when it was time to load up the Mojos would roar into barracks in their huge tank transporters and do the circuit, and as each one passed a tank would fall in behind and follow it round until they were all in. The tanks would then load with much roaring on engines, and then head out straight away, or perhaps camp for the night on the barrack square before making the journey. Our tank drivers went with them in their cabs. The Mojos had their own rank structure and customs and were expert at their job, not surprising perhaps as some had been doing it for well nigh forty years by then. They were also fiends for their schnapps and slivovitz at any time of the day or night and Herculean smokers. As for their food, well, best not ask!

Eventually, after the odd hiccup here and there, personnel and tanks would meet up at Hohne. The tanks would be parked up and guarded on the firing point(s) and the rest of us would pile into our accommodation in the camp proper. To be honest I can't remember much about our living arrangements except it was typically Teutonic, hardly surprising as our predecessors had been at one point the Wehrmacht and Waffen SS tank battalions of Nazi Germany.

It was a matter of pride to get the first round down range as soon as clearance was given to fire at 8.00 am in the morning, weather and range fires permitting. So we got up at some unearthly hour in the morning (my memory says 4.00 am but that can't be right, surely?), had breakfast and were transported out to whatever range we were on in the open backed Stalwart trucks of Motor Transport (MT) troop. Fine, if a bit nippy, if the weather was OK, not so fine if it was raining.

On arriving at the firing point there was a flurry of activity until all was ready. Then we would wait. You always wait in the

army. Sandhurst's motto 'Serve To Lead' was always amended
to 'Rush To Wait' at that gilded institution, and that set the
tone for most of my military career. The RAF transport bods
– Crab Air – were past masters at having their passengers, or
'pax' in Brylcreem Boy-speak, turn up at some unearthly hour
to get their flights, and then making them wait while pilots and
crews had a leisurely breakfast, said goodbye to their boyfriends
and girlfriends, checked out of the hotels where they *had* to
stay otherwise they'd be 'too tired to fly', and amble over to
the airport. How we hated them for their lax, matey, lack of
discipline and regard for their temporary charges.

But I digress. The programme tended to be much the same,
for obvious reasons not least of which was new recruits coming
in all the time. First individual tank static firing, to get the
technicalities right and settle the younger boys down. Then
troop firing, when troop leaders had to control their troops as
multiple targets were popped at the same time. 'Alpha this is
41. Yours on the right, 1500 metres.' 'Ah canny – it's oot o' arc
tae me!' 'Roger, mine then. George, sabot tank on.' 'ON! 1350!'
'1350 FIRE'. 'Firing NOW!' (Bang) 'TARGET!' 'Target, stop.'
'This is 41B – two targets left, 1300 metres.' '41, got them.
Alpha and Bravo split.' And so it went. Exciting stuff, combined
with the 'whoomph' of the 120mm gun and the smell of cordite,
the yelling of the crew over the intercom, and the constant
crackling of the radio from control and the other tanks.

Then we progressed on to battle runs, where we advanced
as a troop down the range towards the targets by bounds and
the gunnery staff popped targets as we went. For this we were
closed down and keeping the troop in line (for safety purposes)

and allocating targets was difficult via narrow vision blocks whilst searching for new targets at the same time. The gun was stabilised in azimuth and elevation so we could shoot pretty accurately on the move, but it made the loader's task all the more dangerous as the breech swung up and down as we bounced down the range. If the staff popped some men-sized targets we then had to shift to engaging with the co-axial machine gun, and the turret would fill with cordite fumes. If you weren't careful they could temporarily asphyxiate your loader and you'd look round to find him unconscious on the turret floor.

There were other incidents. On one occasion one of my troop's tanks was parked with the handbrake off, just as we had de-kitted for maintenance and inspection. The gunner's tank laser sight (TLS), used for ranging and engaging the targets, was laid out on a groundsheet, and of course the tank rolled gently forward and crushed it. A TLS was an expensive piece of kit, many thousands of pounds worth, and I had visions of my salary being docked for the next few years to pay for it. It wasn't my fault, but it was my responsibility. However, after a tense thirty minutes or so one of the boys appeared to tell me 'no' tae worry' because one of the other troops had a 'buckshee', as in spare or free, one and had given it to us. How on earth they came to have a spare piece of kit of that value I didn't dare to ask, but it got me and my troop off the hook.

Dangers aside, however, it was great fun and we were quite good at it. There were always amusing incidents. Every so often someone would get a hang-fire, when instead of a bang as the round went off there would be a fizzing sound, often accompanied by smoke coming out of the breech, as the charge decided whether to go off or not. Usually they went off after a few seconds, but occasionally they didn't go off at all, and then you were into the whole misfire drill followed by a wait of thirty minutes before you could open the breech. This latter event was always approached with a certain amount of trepidation as there was a chance that the inrush of air would set off the charge and it would blow back into the turret and roast everybody in it. Thankfully it never happened in my time, although I did witness a crew so frightened by the hiss and smoke of a hang-fire that they all bailed out and stood on the back deck of their tank, whereupon the gun fired and the round went off downrange. It was the only time I saw an unmanned tank fire.

The ultimate training, however, for us tank soldiers at least, was in Canada, or more specifically at the British Army Training Unit, Suffield (BATUS), in Alberta. BATUS was a remarkable training facility which the British Army had used under licence from the Canadian Government since 1972. It comprised some thousand square miles of prairie in western Canada where, because of lack of population, buildings, and infrastructure, we were free to manoeuvre and fire our weapons almost at will. For a tank troop leader it was the confirmation and testing of competence, a rite of passage between enthusiastic amateur and professional if you like, where every aspect of military skill was applied to a variety of problems set by the staff who were permanently based there. It was also a hurdle at which many commanders and regiments had fallen over the years and, while officially no report was produced to anyone apart from the commanding officers of units who went there, the word soon got out when units and individuals were found wanting.

On average, whilst stationed in Germany as part of 1 (Br) Corps, you might expect to go to Canada once every two years. But you didn't go as a regiment, you went as a BG, an all arms organisation based on a regimental headquarters with all the required bits and pieces from other units tacked on. When I first went to BATUS in 1981 with my troop it was as part of the Scots Guards BG; C and D Squadrons 4th Tanks were their tank support, but it was essentially their exercise.

I rather liked the Scots Guards. True, they were quite different to us in many ways, and their relationship between officers and soldiers was more formal than ours. But they were infantry soldiers and didn't have that extraordinary close bonding that came with serving in a tank crew. In the field I thought they were really, really good. In barracks, in the officers' mess, they had this thing where if you wore your hat at breakfast it signified that you didn't want anyone to talk to you. We thought this was really funny, and went out of our way to engage anyone so attired in conversation, just for the Hell of it. Being Guards officers they indulged us and were endlessly charming and polite. We got on just fine.

I can't actually remember how we got from Germany to Canada the first time, but assume we flew civvy from Dusseldorf to Calgary. It can't have been the RAF since I don't recall any of the delays I had experienced previously, nor do I remember flying backwards across the Pond (RAF transport aircraft had the seats facing backwards at that time); everything seemed to proceed swimmingly. There then followed a bus ride to Camp Crowfoot, the military base near the wonderfully named town of Medicine Hat and from where we would sally forth into the endless prairies on northern Alberta. Plush is not the word that springs to mind in describing our accommodation, but it was fine.

Obviously we didn't take our tanks with us, so we picked up our exercise vehicles at the aptly named dustbowl at Camp Crowfoot, taking them over from the previous BG. There were always some bits and pieces missing from the tanks' equipment, so all sorts of tricks were employed to avoid having to pay for 'diffies'. We did exactly the same when we handed over to the next lot! A BG comprised a lot of vehicles and was a pretty big deal.

Eventually we deployed on to the training area proper, along the Rattlesnake Road if I remember correctly. Then we were out on the prairie living off our tanks for three weeks I think, apart from the occasional shower truck shuttle back to camp for a clean up. Deploying on to the area introduced us to the dust. It was the middle of summer and hadn't rained for months, so each tank threw up a huge plume of dust which got everywhere – mouth, eyes and nose plus other awkward less mentionable spots. It was also frighteningly hot at times – I recorded 116°F (no idea what that is in new money) in the turret on one occasion.

The Canadian prairie is, somewhat paradoxically, both bleak and beautiful. The initial impression of never-ending flatness and loneliness is soon replaced by delight at the fascinating folds and rises of the land; far from being flat, the prairie is crossed by numerous riverbeds, called coulees in this part of the world, and broken by hills and escarpments which hide undiscovered valleys and plains. Most of it is wild grassland, which supports a wide array of wildlife from occasional herds of wild mustangs down to the numerous colonies of gophers, some of which are half tame after being fed by visiting troops over the years. There is also evidence of man's previous occupation of the area in the form of stone rings marking where the native Indians pitched their tepees, usually found in the more sheltered sites or near the rivers.

The usual progression for exercises was followed, troop level followed by squadron/company group with the infantry, and then the whole lot with the BG, involving engineers, artillery, helicopters, old Uncle Tom Cobley and all. The main difference was that we were using real bullets and manoeuvring at the same time, proper fire and movement. The area was so vast that we could really only be a danger to ourselves. Tanks had two white lines painted down either side of the turret and the basic rule of thumb was that, if you saw a target and there was nothing friendly within the arc of the two white lines, you could blast away to your heart's content. We were accompanied by members of the BATUS permanent staff in their Day-Glo painted vehicles who were there mainly to maintain safety, but most of the time we were just left to get on with it.

It had its hairy moments. In those pre-GPS days all navigation was by old-fashioned map reading. A few of the old sweats who'd been in the Middle East back in the day used to talk about using a sun compass, but they were just 'swinging the lamp'. There were virtually no features in the terrain – the very few trees were individually marked – so unless you learned quickly how to read the contours you would become lost. And tanks did get lost, and could pop up anywhere, so you had to be careful. One troop leader was fired at by his squadron leader who mistook his tank for a target. The Discarding Sabot

Training (DST) round, designed to mimic the ballistics of the service round without the same destructive terminal effects, would have gone through the thin armour at the back of the turret had it hit in any case, but luckily his gunner was having an off day. Another exercise was brought to a shuddering halt just as another squadron leader was about to open fire with half his squadron on the other half commanded by his 2ic.

Sadly occasionally there were tragic accidents. On one occasion I remember, an infantry mortar bomb fell short and against all the odds dropped through the open hatch of another vehicle, killing the crew. On another occasion one of the Royal Electrical and Mechanical Engineers (REME) Armoured Recovery Vehicles (ARV) got lost and wandered through a restricted area that had the remnants of mustard gas testing during from the Second World War and the crew received some nasty, but thankfully non-fatal, burns to the legs. But most of the time it was exhilaratingly good fun, and I well remember thinking that there was nothing else in the world I would rather do.

At ENDEX we came off the prairie, repaired the vehicles, cleaned ourselves up and were granted a few days rest and recreation (R&R), of which the less detail the better. Whilst people could, and did, wander further afield, most of the boys spent it locally. The nearest town to Camp Crowfoot, Medicine Hat, was a popular destination. Of particular notoriety was a bar called the Sin Bin which was out of bounds to officers such was its reputation. By all accounts it was dark and cavernous with tables arranged saloon style and waitress service only. It laid on adult orientated entertainment from lunchtime onwards and the floor was always sticky with spilt beer. It was, not to beat about the bush, a bit of a dive. Trouble was not uncommon there, and the Alberta State Police always stationed two or three patrol cars outside in the evening to sort out whatever fracas might develop.

As for me, I took my three weeks annual leave at the end of the exercise and hitch-hiked with a 4th Tanks brother officer, David Eccles, down to San Francisco and back, in the days when you could still do that sort of thing and live. It turned out to be a fascinating road trip through middle America via Montana, Idaho, Nevada and California to reach our ultimate destination of San Francisco. We returned via Oregon and Washington State before cutting back to Alberta through British Columbia. As we hitched our way through the prairie states we were picked up by farmers, a widowed woman with their children who took us to a restaurant and insisted on paying for our meal, and all sorts of travellers who were heading in the right direction.

At night we slept in our sleeping bags in bus shelters, under bridges, or in fields next to whatever road we happened to be travelling at the time. Occasionally we were offered accommodation by those we met, most infamously by three Midwestern girls who took us home to their place after a night at the local bar. I can't remember what happened thereafter, but we stayed more than one night I recall. As we travelled further south towards civilisation the lifts began to dry up and eventually we resorted to the good ol' Greyhound buses which I thought provided an excellent service.

When we arrived in San Francisco we headed straight down to the waterfront and rewarded ourselves, on a lovely sunny day, with oysters and German beers. We had no idea where we were going to stay and harboured some strange notion that we could just turn up at one of the many US military bases there and claim overnight asylum. However, later in the evening, in a bar surprise, surprise, we got talking to an American couple and they very kindly offered us the run of their apartment for as long as we wanted to stay with them, which was incredibly kind of them. So we stayed for a few days with them.

The return journey was fairly uneventful, except we separated at some point and I forged on alone for a while. By now travelling exclusively by bus, I was essentially sleeping rough, which was no big deal after sleeping out on our panzers for the past few weeks. I was, I recall, moved on by the State Police when they found me sleeping on a bench outside a post office, but they drove me to a local camp site and made sure I was all right there. On another occasion, this time in Canada, I met and was taken home for a coffee by a young lady who then told me I had to leave her apartment, which she shared with others, at about midnight, and I had to sleep on top of a picnic table in the local park, but that was OK too. In the end I got back to Calgary and caught my flight back to Germany, so all was well.

Chapter 8

I wouldn't want you to think that the life of a subaltern in the BARITWE was all work and no play, mind. All that *stravaiging* (wandering) around the countryside in big, heavy metal beasts took up only part of our energies, although we spent much more time out of barracks and on our panzers than today's tankies do, by a long shot. Likewise, there did come a point where there was little more to be done on the tank park, our troop sergeant's domain of course. We couldn't spend all our time between exercises painting stones and sweeping leaves otherwise there would have been, quite rightly, a mutiny.

Thank goodness, then, for jollies and adventure training. The former tended to be one-off, *ad hoc* taskings that might be allocated to a junior officer as part of their general military education or, more often, because more senior officers didn't fancy doing them. Examples might be escorting an officer or delegation from a foreign military as they visited the regiment, brigade or division. These tended to be the more boring ones, although if you were a 'thruster' you would welcome the opportunity they sometimes presented to come to the attention of your reporting officer further up the command chain. Others were much more lighthearted and fun; escorting Miss 4 RTR, our chosen young female representative, on her annual visit to the regiment might fall into that category, although officers were usually warned off from becoming too intimately involved with their charges. It did happen though.

Bigger jollies came in a variety of shapes and sizes. The one I was tasked with as a young officer involved taking a Chieftain tank plus crew and support vehicles to the south of France as the UK contribution to the MILAN thermal imaging sight trials. MILAN (Missile d'infanterie léger antichar) was the infantry's standard anti-tank missile at the time, and the newly developed thermal imaging (TI) sight was being trialled by a team from the Infantry Trials and Development Unit (ITDU), based at Warminster. They needed to trial it in all weather conditions, and the wet weather trials were carried out, with us providing the target tank, at Meppen on the North German plain, one of the most depressing places I have ever had the misfortune to visit. It rained non-stop and I had virtually nothing to do, and in the end the tank crew commander, my namesake Corporal Crawford (aka 'Saturday Sanny'), suggested nicely that I should just go back to the barracks in Munster, which I did with some alacrity.

The warm weather trials, on the other hand, were carried out at the French army base near Draguignan, a commune in the Var department in the Provence-Alpes-Côte d'Azur region, in southeastern France, and a mere twenty-six miles inland from St Tropez. 'Haud me back', as we used to say. Getting there was fun. The CO's tank was chosen for the job, together with two REME repair and recovery vehicles and a spare Chieftain power pack, such were the concerns over reliability, and duly departed by rail for the south of France. The route was hardly direct and dictated by the width of various railway bridges along the way, consequently taking several days.

I went with the road party in a couple of land rovers and a four-tonner. It took a long time, given the speed limit restrictions on military vehicles in France, and we did get the odd curious stare from the French police as we made our way south, but it was pretty straightforward. I recall we had an overnight stop with the *75eme Regiment d'Infantrie* in their barracks at Valence (where I think its fair to say we found the food in their canteen interesting) then arrived at Canjuers Camp, at the time the biggest military camp in Europe at 350 square kilometres. Julius Caesar had established the first military presence there during his conquest of Gaul in the first century BC.

Getting the Chieftain up the hill to camp from the railhead was a bit of a nightmare given the narrowness of the road and the steepness of the climb, but we got there in the end after holding up the local traffic for a couple of hours. And once we were there it was pretty relaxed and plain sailing. The Germans, of course, arrived a day after us and just drove their Leopard 1 tank and Marder infantry fighting vehicle (IFV) up the hill with no bother, switched off and went away for lunch. There was not much for me to do when the tank was out on the range being driven up and down for the benefit of the trial, except be in charge. Which was fine. Overall command of the British contingent fell to a major from the Gurkhas, but he was very odd and I spent as little time as I could in his company. His opening address to the assembled team was all about how much trouble they'd be in if they did anything wrong. I had to smooth the waters with my guys afterwards.

We spent an awful lot of time on the beach at St Raphael, which was lovely, and in various little cafés and estaminets in the local area. I learned that escargots Perpignan were not always served in their shells, and that the locals liked their red wine *un peu glacé*. The boys' standard order was 'steak frites wi' a fried oeuf on top an' nae pine needles' – that is no herbs – 's'il vous plait'. We were very polite and had a nice time for several weeks. Getting back to Munster was a bit of an ordeal for the tank crew who travelled by rail with the vehicles. For unknown reasons they got stuck in sidings somewhere for weeks before they finally made it home. The CO went down to visit them wherever they were held up and found the inimitable Corporal Crawford and his crew in fine spirits.

Then there was adventure training, usually referred to as adventure drinking by all. This was (is?) an army wide activity designed to provide energetic and challenging training for those stuck in barracks or in between exercises in the field. The definition of what constituted adventure training was pretty wide, and it was seen primarily as a means for young officers to take their troops or platoons away somewhere different to do something interesting away from the beady eyes of the immediate chain of command. Provided you could persuade your OC or CO that your scheme was a good idea and it fell within the regulations you were on your way.

Many weird and wonderful schemes came to pass under the general banner of adventure training. People went trekking, climbed mountains, learned how to sail, and visited strange locations, and it was a good thing. But inevitably it was open to exploitation and abuse. One famous trip to motorcycle through

Europe and then across the Mediterranean to Morocco and explore the Atlas Mountains got as far as the Cote d'Azur and stayed there, while spurious progress reports were sent back from time to time detailing the rigours of North Africa. Very rarely if ever did anyone check that what had been proposed had actually been carried out, and as long as you submitted a convincing post-exercise report no-one was ever any the wiser.

Such jollies were funded partially from central adventure funds and partly by the individuals participating. There was also the great gift from above that kept on giving, namely 'cash in lieu of rations' or CILOR. Normally soldiers' payment for rations in barracks was deducted at source from their pay; it was subsidised much in the way that meals are subsidised, for example, for MSPs in the Scottish Parliament (and alcohol is too, by the way, but they don't like you to talk about that), but nonetheless payment was made. On adventure training, however, away from barracks, you could apply for CILOR and receive sometimes a considerable sum of money to sustain the troops whilst on their chosen activity. It all had to be accounted for properly, of course, by the expedition leader and I very much doubt if anything underhand happened with the expenditure of funds so received. However, there were always buckshee ration packs in abundance around the barracks and, if all were agreed to exist on this compo for part of the time, there was ample opportunity to use some of the CILOR for other associated activity, if you get my drift. Alternatively, you could agree to starve for a couple of days and then all go to the local restaurant or café for a blow-out, dependent on tastes.

Did adventure training fill its intended remit? I believe it did, and tales of the scrapes and difficulties faced and surmounted on such ventures are legion. Sadly space hardly permits their recounting here, but perhaps another time. They were a welcome part of a young subaltern's life back in the day and an important part of the growing up process in uniform. We had fun, that's for sure. I'll talk about my major adventure training expedition to Pakistan shortly.

Chapter 9

All good things come to an end, and so it was for my all too brief period as troop leader of 13 Troop, D Squadron, 4 RTR. It was time for me to move further up the greasy pole of career progression and I was sent on the Regimental Signals Officer (RSO) course at Bovington Camp in Dorset. The choice was either the RSO course, or the Regimental Gunnery Officer (RGO) course, or the Driving and Maintenance (D&M) course. I wasn't really that interested in gunnery, although my crew could put a DST round through the eye of a needle at 2,000 metres nine times out of ten, nor was I into engines and mechanics. So signals it was.

I will pass on the details of the course except to say I nearly killed myself when my new car skidded on black ice in Poole and sent me careering into a lamppost. An evening in A&E followed, but I was OK and got back in the wee small hours with multiple stitches in an impressive head wound. I was later outraged to get a bill for £540 from the local council for replacing the said lamppost, but luckily my insurance covered it. Back in Germany I took over my new troop.

Command troop was essentially RHQ in the field, transformed into BG HQ for training for operations with additional supporting arms like the RA ('the gunners') or Royal

Engineers (RE) ('the sappers') tacked on. It was the glue that held all the other bits together and tended to cream off the best individuals from the squadrons to man it. Often time spent in command troop was a precursor to promotion so, much as those chosen to join its elitist ranks might squeal about it, they knew that it was a bit of a compliment and would probably lead to greater things.

As an aside, and whether by accident or design I don't know, but all the individuals in command troop – myself included – were really good looking. In fact were often referred to as 'pretty troop' by the envious tank troops and squadrons. Consequently we were always in demand for military displays and the like, and always besieged at them by hordes of attractive young women. In quiet moments of reflection we sometimes used to blame ourselves for being too approachable and available, but we did feel it was our duty to be so. Many of us have continued with this important work in our later careers with considerable success.

Back on track. In the field command troop deployed several vehicles; there was the CO's tank, a couple of Ferret Scout Cars (FSCs), and three Combat Vehicle Reconnaisance (Tracked) (CVR(T)) Sultan command vehicles plus an assortment of other wheeled vehicles. Two of the Sultans were command vehicles proper with various radio rigs, whilst the third was a planning vehicle used by the intelligence and Nuclear, Biological and Chemical (NBC) bods. The Sultans had a pull-out sort of gazebo type arrangement at the back, so you would back up one of the command vehicles with the planning one and make a small, tented area for extra room. If we had the gunners (hawk, spit) or the sappers attached we could form a cruciform arrangement as required. Getting it set up in the middle of the night took some practice, mind.

The other command Sultan would be positioned some way off and would act as 'step up'. In a fast moving tactical scenario where we had to move HQ it would go off to some new location and take over radio control, whereupon the rest of the troop would pack up and move to join them and set up BG HQ again. And so on and so forth. One of the Ferrets was the rebro FSC, commanded in my time by Corporal Scooby Taylor and driven by a trooper known only as 'The Breed'. I initially thought the latter's nickname originated from his penchant for a good, fresh pan loaf, but in fact it related to his alleged similarity to a character in a horror film popular around that time. Anyway, because the very high frequency (VHF) radios we used only operated more or less on line-of-sight, in hilly or urban terrain there could be difficulty communicating with sub units, which is where the rebro came in. It would be sent off at short notice to sit on top of a hill somewhere where it received the command net signal on one set frequency and rebroadcast it on its second set on a different frequency, thereby establishing comms. It worked very well too, though in wartime it would have lasted for about two minutes given the Soviets' direction finding capabilities. Medals all round, though.

Command troop worked really, really hard and being out on exercise could be extremely exhausting. On our first exercise together the CO drove us into the ground, but as soon as he had us working as he wanted he left us alone and dished out the same treatment in turn to the tank squadrons. As ever there were some great characters among the boys and we laughed a lot, even when we were miserable. It would be unfair to single any one member out because they were all great soldiers, but perhaps I should just mention my Troop Sergeant, Peter Reid, who was probably the finest soldier in the field I ever had the good fortune to serve alongside, although there are many other contenders for that title. But he was the one.

Then, suddenly it seemed to me although it had been ages in the planning, we were on our way back to the UK to Tidworth, the historic garrison town on Salisbury Plain. We swapped with the Queen's Royal Irish Hussars (QRIH), a nice enough bunch, handed over everything in Yorke Kaserne to them – including our tanks – and then took over all their stuff in England. Most of this fell upon the Quartermaster (QM) and QM (Tech) and their staffs, plus of course the boys on the tank park. I drove back to Britain halfway through the process with fellow subaltern Alan Dunlop in my new VW Golf GTi, the young officers' car of choice at the time.

Can I just digress here for a minute and explain a classic scam that was being exploited by service personnel, or more specifically young officers, stationed in Germany at that time? As previously mentioned we lived a tax-free existence as far as goods and services were concerned. This applied to new cars, for which we were exempt VAT as well as prices being generally cheaper in Europe than they were in the UK. It didn't take long for some bright spark to work out that you could order a new car tax-free, advertise it for sale in the London papers as you did in those pre-internet times, then drive it back to the UK at the weekend, collect your money from the buyer, than scamper back to Germany by air and pocket a healthy profit.

The scheme was eventually closed down when the BAOR chain of command got wind of what was going on, but some subalterns were doing this every weekend and made a small fortune out of it. It must have been illegal but I don't think anybody got caught.

Anyway, it was a bit odd being back in the UK to be honest. 4th Tanks had been in Munster since 1974 and therefore it took a bit of getting used to initially, but we settled in soon enough. I guess we saw the local area and towns with European eyes and thought them all a bit quaint at first, but that soon passed. With three tank squadrons in Bhurtpore Barracks in Tidworth and A Squadron in Warminster we became 'rent-a-tank' for the UK-based army and spent a lot of time out on Salisbury Plain on various wheezes. Our recce troop in particular seemed to spend more time in the field than it did in barracks.

Having handed over the mighty command troop to another when we moved, I now seemed to have a bewildering succession of jobs in a shortish space of time – 2ic of C Squadron, ops officer in RHQ, even assistant adjutant for about a week until I managed to wriggle out of that one. Much time was spent by everyone catching up on various courses as we were much closer to the various schools that taught our trades and we could fill vacancies at short notice. I went off and completed the Junior Division of Staff College (JDSC) at Warminster, of which I have nothing to report except to say it was mercifully short.

Socially, our lives had changed quite dramatically too. As we were now back home, it was much easier – and cheaper – to travel to see friends and family. Consequently the officers' mess tended to be quiet over the weekend, as did the barracks as a whole. Being orderly officer on a Saturday and Sunday was much more irksome than it had been in Germany, and the possibility of getting awarded extras by the adjutant for some misdemeanour or other was so much more of a powerful threat. On the plus side, it was much easier for us to have visitors and the mess seemed to be frequently full of girlfriends and others. We had some great parties as well. The PoW party we held when we converted the ante room into a prisoners' barrack room in Stalag IV, complete with sandbagged machine gun post and dummies in full German uniform outside the main entrance, was a particularly memorable one. A future CO was noted running into the wall at full speed to demonstrate how effective his German soldiers' helmet was!

There were all sorts of strange things that went on. We brewed our own beer in the mess, a concoction so strong that after two pints you were anybody's. Famously, one of my best friends and lifelong chum, Charlie Pelling, who went on to be my best man and also godfather to my elder daughter, decided he was looking a bit portly (he wasn't really) and that he should go on a diet. He then designed his own diet, which consisted of giving up food altogether and drinking beer at every meal instead, breakfast, lunch, and dinner. I'd like to be able to say this went on for six months, but in reality he managed to sustain it for about a fortnight, which I thought was pretty good going myself. It worked too, for the pounds fell off, and he was undoubtedly the happiest dieter I have ever met during it.

Our local pub of choice was the White Horse at Thruxton just next to the famous racing circuit. We could be found there any day of the week but for some reason Tuesday evenings became the standard fixture. I have many a memory of being driven back to the mess after closing time at breakneck speed through narrow Wiltshire lanes by friends who might not have passed the breathalyser test had they been asked. There was little traffic on those roads, however, and the boys in blue clearly had better things to do. Although there was the odd shunt, including Charlie famously parking his MG sports car vertically up a tree trunk by the side of the road, we all survived more or less intact, thank goodness. Philip Warner even woke up one morning, having slept fully clothed in the rose garden outside his rented cottage, with the engine of his rather racy Ford Escort XR3i still running and the driver's door open. What a good time we had!

Chapter 10

One of the major events I organised and took part in whilst 2ic of C Squadron in Tidworth involved taking a number of soldiers adventure training to Pakistan. I was never quite sure whether it was meant to be a jolly for me, or because I had got the whole squadron lost in the middle of the night on Salisbury Plain a few weeks before. There was no GPS in those days, of course, and map reading with minimal light in that moonscape was no picnic. I had ended up having to walk ahead of my tank with a compass to get us back, but the one consolation was that nobody else knew where we were either.

Anyhoo, our CO at the time had decided that all squadrons under his command should carry out adventure training, and that C Squadron should visit our long lost cousins the 13th Lancers in Pakistan. My squadron leader, Andrew Hill, told me to crack on and that was about as much direction as I got. And so Exercise Tartan Trek was born from humble beginnings. Now, back in 1983 there was no internet nor mobile phones and communications by telephone to the Indian subcontinent tenuous at best, so we corresponded with our Pakistan army colleagues by signal, a sort of modernised telegraph system. It seemed to work fine initially and we were told we were welcome to visit.

Our knowledge of Pakistan was limited at best, but we knew the 13th Lancers were based in Lahore, and I think we used a school atlas to find out exactly where that was. However, to justify the 'adventure' bit of adventure training we had to find something mildly challenging and strenuous to do. Someone, and I have no idea who, suggested we go trekking up the Swat Valley in the north-east of the country, so we found it on the map and agreed that would be the plan. I think we expected it to be a bit like Glencoe but maybe a bit warmer but we didn't really have a clue.

Well, everyone knows about the Swat Valley these days. It's where all the bad guys are – Mujahadeen, Taliban, Al-Quaeda, ISIS, you name 'em, that's where they all hang out. It's a bit like the fabled Badlands of Wild West fame but infinitely more dangerous. Jesse James and his gang would have taken one look and thought 'nah, bit dodgy mate'. But in our ignorance we thought it would be safe as houses and thought no more about it.

Having got the go-ahead to proceed, the first problem was getting there. Clearly we would have to fly, but in those pre-internet days you couldn't just book online. However, there were these things called bucket shops where airlines dumped their surplus tickets at a discounted price. My 2ic for the trip, Niall Macnaughton, took upon himself the task of purchasing the cheapest tickets he could find, and eventually returned from London with the tickets in hand. We were to fly from London to Karachi and then on to Lahore.

Eventually approximately fifteen C Squadron personnel left Tidworth for Heathrow and then on to Karachi. I remember nothing of the journey at all except that when we disembarked to change planes the heat hit us like a wall. In fact one of the boys said 'it must be the heat from the engines' as we disembarked. I was also mildly surprised that there was no-one to meet us, but thought we would be received by our hosts at our final destination, Lahore. However, when we got to Lahore airport there was nobody to meet us there either, and I began to suspect that something was amiss. We had arrived in Pakistan and nobody seemed to know, or to care. Classic young officer challenge.

So Niall and I left the boys at the airport, hailed a cab, and went to search out our hosts. It being the middle of the day and very warm, Lahore was deserted and we soon enough got to the relevant barracks. All was still as we walked into the RHQ of the 13th Lancers and the only living thing, apart from their very smart guards, was their adjutant, sitting in civvies at his desk and catching up on his paperwork. As we knocked at his door and entered he looked up and said something like; 'Oh no, I do hope you are not our visitors from the UK!' We told him that indeed we were, and it transpired he knew we were coming but just not when. Our last couple of signals had gone adrift.

Anyway, a few swift phone calls and all was sorted. We went back for the boys with transport and found them already being looked after by our hosts. After this unplanned beginning things went smoothly, and we were looked after very well and with great kindness. Aside from some local sightseeing and a tour of some other military units in the Lahore cantonment, Niall and I did a couple of journeys by internal Pakistan International Airline (PIA) flights for more official visits. By the way, did you know that all in-flight meals on PIA are curried? Anyway, for example, we went up to Peshawar to visit General Lhodi, who commanded their 4 Corps and who gave us a detailed briefing on the operational situation in his command. Remember, at this time the Soviets were just across the border in Afghanistan.

Eventually we made our way up to the Swat Valley, via the Khyber Pass, where we intended to do a bit of trekking. The Pakistan Armoured Corps (PAC) had a hut – more of a bungalow – at Kalam, where we stayed three nights. Our hosts couldn't understand why we wanted to walk up the valley as they were perfectly happy to drive us instead. What we probably didn't fully understand was that we were literally in bandit country, which explained why they insisted we had a full platoon of fully armed infantry accompanying us all the time we were up there! Ignorance is bliss, as they say, and we were ignorant of the dangers.

We also visited the Chitral Scouts regiment at their HQ at Drosh Fort at the top of the valley close to the border with Afghanistan. They entertained us most generously in that remote location, and we played them, and lost heavily, at football, partly because we were at considerable altitude and the boys were quickly gasping for breath. Their soldiers were fully acclimatised and as fit as fiddles and I think they graciously took their foot off the gas when they saw us floundering and kept the score line fairly respectable. They also put on a polo match for us, as spectators not participants thank goodness, which was pretty spectacular given the setting. Plus we were encouraged to join in with their regimental tribal dancing, which we did. Sadly I have no photographs of this with which to embarrass my former soldiers. Corporal John Fyfe, I'm looking at you.

In retrospect our trip to Swat wasn't at all physically demanding as I think we'd hoped it might be, mainly because our hosts insisted on driving us most of the way, but in terms of being adventurous it most certainly was. Historically, though, we weren't the first westerners to go there, not by a long chalk. Alexander the Great and his armies had swung past centuries before, and it was remarkable to meet the blue-eyed, blond-haired Kalash people, quite unlike neighbouring tribes in appearance, who are reckoned to be the descendants of that incursion so long ago.

I can't remember too much of our journey back to the UK, except when exiting Pakistan we were temporarily halted by a particularly evil looking customs official who suspected we were carrying drugs (we travelled in civvies). The minute I said we were there as guests of the Pakistan Army he scuttled away with profuse apologies and we proceeded without further ado. The rest of the homeward journey was unremarkable.

Back in Tidworth we got back into the swing of things and were surprised to find that, despite having been away for only three weeks or so, we were quite unfit and had trouble keeping up with the regular regimental runs. But we got over that and that was that. One of the boys, Lance Corporal Alex McKnight I think it was, had also picked up a particularly nasty bacterial disease called Shigella, which made him quite ill for some time after our return until the tropical medicine boys at the RAF Wroughton hospital worked out exactly what was wrong with him, whereupon he recovered.

Did the trip qualify as adventure training? Undoubtedly so, for we had not only visited our long lost sister regiment the 13th

Lancers and represented the British army, but had also been exposed to sights, sounds, smells and challenges which most of us had not experienced before, and I dare say many of us will not have experienced again. One of the other RTRs repeated the visit a few years later and it was a much more official and well organised operation than our pioneering effort in 1983. They were met by official hosts on arrival with much saluting and uniforms in evidence, and no bad thing. But I still have a fondness for the way we did it, warts and all.

Chapter 11

During my military career I was involved in two major military operations; the biggest by far was the First Gulf War 1990-91, of which more in Chapter 16. The other was Exercise Lionheart in 1984, which was also quite staggering in scale. Lionheart was a test and demonstration of 1 (Br) Corps ability to deploy and meet a massed Soviet attack across the Inner German Border (IGB) during the Cold War, and involved some 131,000 British troops, including Territorial Army and reservists from Germany and the UK, and took place over 3,700 square miles in Belgium, the Netherlands and (then) West Germany. A further 3,500 Dutch, 6,300 German, 3,400 US and 165 Commonwealth soldiers also took part as enemy and umpires amongst other functions. It was a huge effort.

The regiment was still stationed at Tidworth on Salisbury Plain as part of 19 Infantry Brigade, which itself was part of the 3rd UK Armoured Division on deployment. The exercise comprised two main parts: Exercise Full Flow, which practised the deployment of UK-based elements across the Channel to Ostend or Zeebrugge and then into position alongside Germany based elements, followed by the combat training bit which was called Exercise Spearpoint.

In some ways the deployment part was the most interesting for us. The panzers went by road (transporter, I assume) to the little known military port of Marchwood near Southampton, there to be loaded on to one or other of the Royal Fleet Auxiliaries (RFAs) and shipped over to Zeebrugge. Of this move I know nothing as I went with the road party, travelling in CO Hedley Duncan's landrover as I was then ops officer. I think we went by civillian ferry to Ostend.

Upon arrival we disembarked and then were directed to a section of the Belgian motorway system which had been blocked off to civvy traffic to allow us to form up into groupings for the journey into West Germany. Here we were marshalled by the RMP and Belgian police into 'packets' of vehicles and eventually sent on our way along the motorway system towards the German border. Thousands of vehicles proceeded at a maddeningly slow pace – forty kilometres in the hour or something like that – all day and all night.

Once across the border into Germany we entered a replen area. In real conflict we would have, of course, deployed upon multiple routes via numerous replen stops, but such arrangements in peacetime would have been overly disruptive. Be that as it may, our replen area provided fuel for the vehicles, a chance for a wash and shave, and a hot meal. It was run by one of the Royal Irish Ranger (RIR) battalions, and faced with the challenge of feeding the thousands arriving around the clock, they had made the very sensible decision to provide one menu only, in vast quantities, twenty-four hours a day. So, for breakfast, lunch, and dinner the choice was ... Irish stew. And very good it was too.

I can't remember the details of where and when we married up with our panzers, but we then deployed into hides as we would have done for real. 4 RTR BG at this point consisted of RHQ, C Squadron, G Squadron, and a mechanised infantry company from 1 Staffords, having exported our other squadrons to other BGs within 19 Infantry Brigade, our parent formation initially. In BG HQ we established ourselves right in the middle of a typically neat German rural town, hiding our vehicles away in barns and farmyards occupied by the local population who didn't seem at all fazed by our invasion into their privacy. C Squadron leader, Major Tom Brown US Army (on attachment), chose to take his tanks and hide them in a wood a few kilometres away, probably to get as far away from RHQ as possible!

Having settled in, 'cammed up', and established our routine, we waited, a not unusual occurrence in military manoeuvres. I think we waited for a week at least with not much happening. Then the exercise enemy started probing. I have recollections of being unable to get permission from brigade to engage a broadside-on enemy at ideal range because they couldn't get authority from division, a grim reminder of the lack of confidence and ability to react quickly that has plagued the British army since time immemorial. By the time brigade gave the OK they were long gone into our rear areas.

Finally, I was woken in the middle of the night by orange flashing lights to find we had been over-run by the Americans. They had taken us completely by surprise with their speed, movement, and guile, and we had been caught with our trousers down, so to speak. All I could do was wake up the CO, and we bugged out Hell for leather towards the rear. Not a very auspicious beginning to our exercise and a salutary lesson that we had to think and act quicker.

This was phase one of the exercise, defending against the enemy attack. Phase two was, as ever, the counter attack and drive to final victory. At some point we got our other two tank squadrons back, crossed the River Leine (thank goodness the CO and I had done a recce the night before otherwise we would never have found the crossing point!) and advanced to Sibbesse where we were regrouped into 20 Armoured Brigade for the final part of the exercise. One of the more interesting parts of proceedings was casualty evacuation procedures, which we practised as if real. Inevitably some of our tanks broke down, and others were designated casualties by the exercise umpires. These were then recovered by standard operating procedures, but we didn't see the crews again for weeks and some of the panzers were only returned to us months later.

Of our return to the UK I can recall very little, except that bizarrely we staged through our old barracks at York Kaserne in Munster, now occupied by the QRIH. They were, how shall I put it, grudgingly hospitable towards us, and put a brave face on hosting their clearly unwelcome guests. Compare and contrast with the wonderful Seventeen-Slash-Two-One-Ell (17/21st Lancers) who were still just down the road where we had left them when we moved to the UK. I went down to see my old chums and was immediately invited to one of their formal officers' mess dinner nights. I protested that I only had my combat kit to wear but was told that was immaterial. Accordingly I found myself their guest, my hosts in their very fine mess kit, silver on the table and regimental band playing through dinner, with me in my combats. The band even played the march of the RTR in my honour as their guest. There's the mark of a professional and confident regiment!

After a few days we were on our way, and this time I came back with the CO's party together with some of our tanks on one of the RFAs, possibly *Sir Bedivere* or one of its ilk. On our way across the Channel it blew up a Force 9 gale, which is pretty rough actually, and we were forced to hold off from docking at Marchwood until the storm passed. Luckily for us, a nip of gin in the officers' wardroom was two pence at the time, and I don't think any of us were bothered by the weather at all! The next day we docked and were soon back in Bhurtpore Barracks in Tidworth, with most of the rest of the regiment rejoining us in the next couple of days.

And that was it, probably the biggest peacetime exercise the British army undertook in recent memory. There was no hanging about, though, for 4th Tanks was coming to the end of its UK sojourn and was due to head back to West Germany, exchanging barracks with the 5th Inniskilling Dragoon Guards (5 Innis DG) in Osnabruck, not far from our previous home in Munster. I suspect most of the boys were happy to return to Germany where the pay was better and the standard of living probably higher at that time. Many of us found life in an English garrison town a tad monotonous and were glad when it came to an end.

I, however, did not return overseas with the Regiment, as I had passed the staff college exams and was selected to start that two year episode almost immediately. I was not to return to 4th Tanks, apart from a couple of short visits, for another four years.

Chapter 12

4th Tanks had gone back to West Germany and I was on my own. As I said, I had been accepted for the army staff college, which was quite a big deal actually. It was a watershed in any army officer's career. If you got to staff college you were on the way up. If you didn't, well, you either resigned your commission and left or accepted the fact that you were never going to command an armoured brigade or division but that was OK; being a soldier was what fired your rockets and rank and status was not so important. I sympathise completely with this view.

But I had got in. All my pals had assumed that I would get to go to staff college because I had an Oxbridge degree but that was just an additional burden. Some of the guys I knew had school qualifications only but they seemed to be much better army officers than me. Dammit, some of my soldiers might have made better army officers than me! People expected me to get in and that made the whole examination process more stressful, but I passed. Blessed relief.

In those days the staff college course was, for me at least, a full two years; the first year was to be spent at the Royal Military College of Science (RMCS) at Shrivenham, Oxfordshire, and the second year at the Army Staff College (ASC), Camberley, in Surrey. I went home to stay with my folks over the 1985/86 Christmas holidays, and then, as was regimental practice as I knew it, left to start the course at Shrivenham at the last safe moment, driving down and changing into my uniform in a motorway service station on the way. I parked my car on the parade square when I arrived and walked into the commandant's course opening address in the main auditorium with about five minutes to spare.

That's precisely the moment when I realised I had got it wrong. Almost every one of my fellow students had been there for weeks, settling in and catching up on their pre-course reading. It seemed that the carefree days of regimental soldiering had lulled me into a false sense of security and that now things were a bit more serious. On top of this, about ninety per cent of my new compadres were married and many had children; there was just a handful of single officers attending, a far cry from the twenty-five odd single subalterns that had inhabited the 4th Tanks officers' mess but a few months before. Turning up at the last minute with all your possessions in the back of the car wasn't normal behaviour any more. Time to grow up.

I had been allocated a room in the officers' mess but from the first night I knew I didn't want to stay there, so I sought out like-minded bachelors who might fancy living in rented accommodation off campus. Having teamed up with a para and a gunner (hawk, spit), we found an isolated farmhouse just outside Wootton Bassett and rented it from the family who were living temporarily in Japan. It was an old, brick-built, ugly building, freezing cold in winter, called Bincknoll House. As the first part of our course was statistics, it quickly became known as 'Binomial' House, although I still don't have a clue what a binomial is when it's at home.

The Shrivenham course was pretty dire and uninspiring and I can't say I enjoyed it much. I decided early on that I wasn't really interested in competing and so aimed to graduate right in the middle of the class. In this I was helped by the new adoption of computers which RMCS Shrivenham was in some ways an early pioneer. Everyone, staff and pupils, seemed to use their wife's first name as their password and so checking one's grading mid-course was 'easy peasy, lemon squeezy' and one could adjust one's academic effort accordingly. I passed right on the fifty per cent mark in comparison with my course mates. Job done.

The second year was at the ASC which was located in the RMA Sandhurst campus, an altogether more prestigious and career defining rite of passage. My erstwhile para and gunner (hawk, spit) housemates had decided that they would prefer to live in bachelor accommodation within the college, so I found a couple of other colleagues and rented a house in nearby Crowthorne, an aspirational middle-class new build property, where the family was going abroad for the year. It was fine.

Of the course itself perhaps the less said the better, and I didn't like the ultra-competitive atmosphere at all. We seemed to spend much time in the nearby countryside, waving our arms around and pointing at imaginary enemies and hypothetical solutions to military problems. I recall I once sited my (pretend) infantry anti-tank missiles in Sarah Ferguson's father's garden in the village of Dummer, and also planned the demolition of the bridge over the Thames at Wallingford. All in a day's work, then back for tea. I was also aware, for the first time really, that some of my fellow students were real thrusters, ambitious individuals for whom nothing could be allowed to get in the way of their single-minded quest for personal career advancement.

There were two things, however, which made the experience palatable. The first was that, as students at the ASC, we became eligible for membership of Wentworth Golf Club at a mere twenty-five per cent of the normal membership subscription for the time of our course. Why this was so escapes me, but I suspect that it was a valiant attempt by the club committee to add a little tone to its otherwise mainly *nouveau riche* and *arriviste* membership. The golf courses themselves were magnificent and well beyond my golfing capabilities most of the time. The clubhouse was also well used by us but I think we thought the rest of the members to be, well, a little bit vulgar if I'm honest? Wentworth had a 'guid conceit o' itself' which we did not necessarily share. Perhaps it is different nowadays.

My greatest joy, however, was to become editor of the college annual magazine, *Owl Pie*. I had been dabbling in writing short articles for regimental and other assorted military journals for a while, and indeed had been instrumental in putting out the unauthorised but tolerated scurrilous newsletter during my time at Shrivenham. But *Owl Pie* was an official publication and accordingly a much more powerful and influential magazine. Just the opportunity for me!

Since the mid-eighteenth century the annual editions of the magazine had been produced along conventional military journal lines and bound in plum coloured leather bindings with gold stamped lettering on the cover. I decided to revamp the presentation, and settled on a spoof cover mimicking *Punch* magazine, warning from my lawyer friends about breach of copyright and trademarks notwithstanding. And that's what we did, with articles written by me and a broad spectrum of my colleagues and illustrated with some rather splendid cartoons by Sebastian Roberts (later Major General of this parish). And, when I last looked, some time ago now I'll admit, successor editors followed the same model, at least until the ASC closed in 1997 and amalgamated with the equivalent institutions of the RN and RAF in the Joint Service Command and Staff College (JSCSC).

I can't claim to have enjoyed my two years on the two staff courses, rather I *tholed* them if I can use that Scottish term. It wasn't an unpleasant experience, nor was it something I'd be happy to repeat. It had to be done, and it was. Plus I got promoted to major whilst I was there which helped with the bills. At the end of the course we were all allocated our future jobs via the 'black bag' (no, I have no idea either) appointments process. Some went back to regimental duty, some went off to staff jobs. Having spent a year at Shrivenham undertaking a technical education I had indicated that I would prefer to do a 'weapons' job, and I found myself posted to Bovington in Dorset, the same place I had done my troop leader's and regimental signals officer's courses previously. I couldn't have planned it better if I had tried.

Chapter 13

As I said, after two years at staff college I had been given my very first staff job ever at the Headquarters of the Director of the Royal Armoured Corps (HQ DRAC) down in delightful Dorset. I had no idea what this organisation did or how it fitted in to the bigger picture, but I was just mightily relieved not to be posted to the MoD in London which would have been total anathema to me. In fact, I devoted some time and effort to avoiding being posted to London, because the word on the streets on working there was all bad. Early starts, long days, ambitious superiors, and precious little down time. Dorset was altogether a more gentle and relaxed environment and suited me down to the ground.

My official job title in typical MoD-speak gobbledy-gook was SO2 RAC 2a, which meant nothing to me when I got my posting but which transpired to involve representing HQ DRAC's views on future RAC equipment procurement. It was, therefore, more or less exactly what I'd been looking for, and I found myself working in a very relaxed HQ with a nice general in charge and sharing an office with the delightful Robin Goldsmith of the 17/21 L, my favourite cavalry regiment. Both of us were mildly maverick in outlook and so we got on very well.

But first I had to get my accommodation sorted out. The officers' mess at Bovington was a classic example of all that was wrong with 1960s architecture and was rather like a tower block in a sink estate. Whilst busy during the week and comfortable enough, the weekends saw it deserted and a soulless and a depressing place to be far from home. So I needed to find somewhere else, and fast. I answered an advertisement on the notice board and found myself in a small flat in the nearby town of Wareham at 59 Roper's Lane, but whilst comfortable enough it was only ever a temporary measure while I scouted out some of the very lovely properties for rent in the Dorset countryside.

After being turned down when I applied for an apartment in one of the local manor houses, probably because the owners didn't consider me smart enough to match their social aspirations, I was lucky enough to be able to rent a thatched cottage in the miniscule village of Moreton, a stone's throw from my new office. It had three bedrooms which meant I could have shared it with others, but I decided I wanted to live there on my own. It wasn't very grand at all, although it had an Aga in the kitchen, and was freezing in winter, but I liked it a lot. Lots of friends came to stay over my two year time there, but I was the only permanent fixture resident-wise.

Perhaps the most notable thing about Moreton is that it is the final resting place of T E Lawrence, aka Lawrence of Arabia. He had been killed in motorcycle accident in 1935 whilst stationed with the RTC at Bovington (as a private soldier, although he had been a colonel in his desert days) and living in the cottage known as Clouds Hill, now run by the National

Trust (NT). Many a time I visited both his grave and cottage, hoping perhaps for some military inspiration. Moreton church also had some lovely engraved glass windows by Whistler, and was apparently bombed by the Luftwaffe in 1941 when they were trying to hit the camp. Bomb aiming was clearly not their strongest suit back then.

Aside from the tiny post office and general store directly opposite my cottage, plus a few other buildings in similar vein, there wasn't much else in the village to capture the attention, apart from its general rural charm. Just a mile or so down the road, though, lay the Seven Stars pub, which became a frequent and popular place of gathering for like minded souls like me. Many an evening there passed pleasantly enough over a bottle or two of their renowned Steam Beer, which came from a brewery in Newquay if I remember correctly. Sadly, they don't seem to brew it any more but it was powerful stuff. My regimental chum Iain Willis took up residency there whilst doing his RSO's course and our mutual pal Charlie Pelling used to travel down of a weekend after his weekly stint at the MoD, so we had many a lively evening there. Of course I never drove home via the deserted country roads afterwards.

My job was really interesting and I thoroughly enjoyed doing it. The biggest project by far during my time there was the Chieftain replacement project; our old tanks had already been up-armoured a couple of years before when we realised – oops – that its armour would no longer keep out the most modern iteration of Soviet tank gun ammunition, as the Iran-Iraq War of 1980-88 had amply demonstrated. But the old girl was now at the end of the road and we needed something newer and better. I have written elsewhere about how I think the eventual replacement chosen, Challenger 2, was the wrong choice, and there's no need to repeat it all again here. It's just a bit galling to note that the current proposed Life Enhancement Programme for Challenger 2 in its turn may include some of the items that we recommended in the first place, some thirty-five years ago!

The problem seemed to me to be, if you'll allow me one of those sweeping generalisations of which I am so inordinately fond, that the senior officers making the decisions weren't nearly half as clued up on technical matters as we Young Turks out of staff college were, and they were easily impressed and swayed by those they deemed senior and more important than us. At least our general had the decency to call us 'his Young Turks' but he still didn't follow our recommendation on this one. Hey ho.

There were a myriad of other equipment programmes which crossed our decks, too many for me to remember most of them. I do recall the Bowman tactical communications system (radios to you and me) upon which we worked and was due in service in 1988, so we were told. It actually entered service in 2004, hugely delayed and hugely over budget because people couldn't make their minds up, and accordingly verging on obsolete when it arrived with the troops.

Tank heaters were another, minor, project. Chieftain and Challenger1 tanks had no heaters in them and consequently a concomitant part of being a tank soldier was to spend most of your time on the panzers freezing to death. Believe it or not, one of the reasons the procurement of heaters was resisted by the hierarchy was the fear that 'they might make the boys go soft'. A better argument was that they might glow in the dark, and indeed in the light, when the opposition turned their TI sights on them, which was probably fair enough. Another flawed argument militated against body armour for tank soldiers ('because they have armour already, stupid') which sadly had fatal consequences for one RTR commander much later in Iraq.

Occasionally I had to attend meetings at the MoD in London, which called for an early start from the little rail station at Wool in Dorset. Every time I went I thanked the Lord I had never been pinged for a London staff post. The meetings were in general interminably long and seldom reached any firm conclusions; held in a cloud of cigarette smoke in a grey, scruffy office in a grey, dilapidated block round the back of a railway station. Fun they were not and I couldn't wait to get back to sleepy Bovington. I also sometimes accompanied the general in some of his visits to various units of the RAC as they fired on the nearby Lulworth Ranges, with much saluting, crashing of boots, and nervous bonhomie involved.

Defence budgets were always tight, as they still are nowadays, and we were forever being asked to find savings in existing programmes to help fund others. The usual methodology for this was to spread the payments for various bits of kit over a longer timeframe, which might fix the annual budget figures but usually meant the total expense was greater. Then, counter-intuitively, around the end of the financial year in February/March, a harassed MoD staff officer would phone and ask if there was anything we could think of quickly that we wanted as the budget was underspent! If you didn't spend your annual budget it might get cut the next year. What a way to run an operation, but I suspect it was ever thus and probably still is. Don't let the taxpayer find out, that's all I will say.

I have to admit, though, that I really did enjoy my time in Dorset, and I also think the job I did was a useful one. My colleagues and I didn't always get our points across or our views accepted, but I certainly didn't think our efforts were in vain. At the end of the day, we did our best to ensure the RAC got the best equipment it could get in straitened financial circumstances. I was able to apply many of the lessons learned there when I returned to a similar job in an operational headquarters during the First Gulf War, but that's for a later chapter. My two year stint was up all too quickly, but I looked forward to rejoining the regiment in my new role as squadron leader. After four years away I was keen to get back.

Chapter 14

When I rejoined 4th Tanks in early 1989 it was still in Osnabruck. I had visited the regiment once, I think, over the past four years and it was less familiar to me although only some of the personalities had changed. The officers' mess, though, was quite different. A whole generation of young subalterns had joined, and many had already left having completed their SSCs, during the time I had been away. I also found that I was now the most senior bachelor officer which was distinctly odd.

The good news was that the regiment was now commanded by Lieutenant Colonel (later Brigadier) Charlie McBean, a fellow Glaswegian, and his adjutant was another Scotsman, Archie Lightfoot from South Uist, so we really did live up to our claim of being 'Scotland's Own Royal Tank Regiment'. I was given command of C Squadron, where my 2ic was Patrick Kidd, who went on to become a brigadier in the Australian army, and the subalterns were Hamish De Bretton-Gordon (now the media's go-to expert on all aspects of chemical and biological warfare), Sean Rickard, a Kiwi, Charlie Pratt (now Cavanagh), and Brett Fleming-Jones. They were all nice boys and I liked them a lot. I think Patrick probably thought I was a bit casual and a soft touch discipline wise, and he may have been right. After all, he's the one that made brigadier, not me!

It's an old adage that the senior NCOs were, and no doubt still are, the backbone of the British army, and that was definitely the case in C Squadron. Mine were an outstanding bunch; I couldn't have wished for a better Squadron Sergeant Major (SSM) than Stuart King, nor in my SQMS Davy Valley. Troop sergeants came and went a little during my time in command but included John Barnwell, Sinky Sinclair, Jimmy Simpson (now McCalman), John Riach, Murdo McLeod and Jack Russell. They were the ones who kept the whole thing ticking over smoothly and were a fine bunch.

I arrived back at the regiment just in time to participate in our United Nations (UN) tour of Cyprus as dismounted infantry. This was meant to be a jolly, a holiday posting for all of us after eight years of BAOR grind on panzers. Consequently, in early 1989 we put our tanks into the hangars and started re-learning the basic infantry skills we had all gone through in basic training. Out went our Sterling sub-machine guns (SMGs) and in came the Belgian designed self-loading rifles (SLRs), bigger, longer, heavier and infinitely more powerful. They allowed the old sweats to swing the lamp about previous Nor'n Ireland tours where they had last used them.

4th Tanks had always been reasonably fit; we held two regimental runs a week on top of other voluntary sports activities. Now we commenced trying to get *infantry* fit with a series of route marches carrying rifles and webbing, and it was surprising how many of the younger lads found this difficult. We got there in the end, though. Then at some point we had to pass our Annual Personal Weapon Test (APWT) on the SLR. The final bit of preparation was the CO's exercise to confirm our infantry skills in a series of advances, attacks, and patrols out in the field.

The field, in this case, was literally that, German farmers' fields in the monotonously boring northwest German plain. Depressing at the best of times in late winter/early spring, they were made much worse by the near constant rain and the farmers' habit of spreading untreated pig manure on them as fertiliser to encourage crop growth. As the correct response to coming under effective enemy fire is 'down, crawl, observe, fire', you can imagine how popular that was in the circumstances. We stank to high Heaven and were only too glad when it ended.

And then in June of that year we went. I can't actually remember how we got there but obviously we flew. I do remember the CO getting mightily hacked off with the RAF for making us wait around for some considerable time before we set off, a recurring theme during my military career. We *hated* RAF movements, who we thought lax, scruffy, rude and inefficient – which they were. Anyway, eventually we landed in RAF Akrotiri and wended our way up to Dhekelia in the Sovereign Base Area (SBA), where C Squadron was to spend the first three months of our six month tour before moving up on to the UN Green Line.

Soldiering in the SBA was like being back in the days of the Empire. We were nominally guarding the base, but in fact there was no enemy, and the boys got quickly bored stagging on (being on guard duty) despite a few training exercises thrown in to keep us occupied. The base commander was clearly bonkers, perhaps having spent too long in the sun. It was his habit to turn up at 3.00 am in the wee small hours in full dress uniform to inspect the pillboxes our sentries manned 24/7, probably to try and catch them sleeping on the job. We despised him for it.

It was blooming hot too, and we worked from 6.00 am until 2.00 pm and then packed it in for the day. Our barracks were on the beach, and for the first fortnight the sea was full of white, skinny Scottish soldiers frolicking about as if on holiday in Torremolinos. After that initial burst of enthusiasm few bothered any more. We spent time at the nearby Larnaca 'strip', a collection of dingy and dilapidated bars, restaurants and clubs which ran along the coast road, and dined on a standard and repetitive menu of mezes (a selection of small dishes served as appetizers) until we could stand them no more. In the officers' mess brandy sours were the drink of the tour for reasons I know not – cheap brandy I would presume. They were very refreshing anyway.

To be frank, southern – that is Greek – Cyprus was a mess at that time, all dusty roads and half finished buildings with the beginnings of the modern tourist trade which now defines it. The British expats were awful people and we tried to have as little to do with them as we could. The British holidaymakers were even more so. I did spend some time, though, visiting some of the ancient ruins on the island which were quite impressive. There was also a rolling programme for R&R which meant that we were never completely up to strength at any one time. Lots of the boys took the boat trip to Egypt, which by all accounts was a bit of a booze cruise, whereas the officers tended to go home or bring their WAGs over to the island for a fortnight or longer.

At some point we went up the long, narrow extension to the SBA which led up to the listening station at Ayios Niklaos, just short of the deserted former holiday resort of Famagusta which was in the middle of the no-man's land between Turkish and Greek Cypriots. What allegedly goes on here can be found via Wikipedia but suffice to say there seemed to be a large number of civilian employees on site and in the officers' mess there, many of whom seemed to be Arabic speakers. I can't for the life of me think why that should have been the case, but there you go.

The six odd weeks we spent there were doubly dull. The boys once again stagged on guarding the barracks and manning a check point that led into nowhere and whose traffic mainly consisted of locals going to their fields. There was yet another dingy roadside restaurant serving the local fare there and not much else. I think it would be fair to say that we were pretty bored there, even more bored than we had become back down in Dhekelia. It was tedious in the extreme.

How to sum up our time spent in the SBA at Dhekelia? After the initial frisson of excitement of the new it was pretty humdrum. We were there because we were there, but it certainly didn't turn out to be the holiday posting we imagined. In our boredom and ignorance we were almost looking forward to going up on to the Green Line as part of the UN. We should have been more careful about what we wished for, but that was about to become abundantly clear to us.

Halfway through our six month tour, then, we moved up to the UN Green Line and put on our blue berets – we were UN soldiers now! By way of background, the United Nations Buffer Zone in Cyprus ran across the middle of the island from west to east and separated the previously warring Greek Cypriots to the south from the Turkish Cypriots in the north in the self-declared Turkish Republic of Northern Cyprus (TRNC). It varied in depth from a few metres in the middle of Nicosia to nearly five miles in some of the rural areas, and was commonly called the Green Line. If you want more detail as to how it came into being then Wikipedia is as good a source as any.

C Squadron's tactical area of responsibility (TAOR) ran from just outside of Nicosia for about thirteen kilometres to the west and was mainly rural in nature with a few villages scattered here and there, and our orbat (order of battle) consisted of about a hundred blokes all told at various times. My squadron headquarters (SHQ) was in an abandoned and semi-derelict primary school which still bore the pockmarks of small arms fire from the 1974 fighting. I had my own small room there which gave me a modicum of privacy and we all got on well in SHQ. The dereliction surrounding us could be a bit oppressive at times but the weather was generally good and blue skies have an important psychological impact. We were fine.

My three troops were scattered across our TAOR and were to all intents and purposes semi-autonomous. It was in many ways classic young officer stuff redolent of the days of Empire; young subalterns on their own with their boys in the *ulu* (Malay, to describe a place that is remote or deserted) and responsible for everything that happened there. To the north was the

Turkish army and to the south the Greek Cypriot National Guard (GCNG) had their positions, from where both sides glared at each other with us in the middle.

Our job was to patrol the buffer zone and keep the two antagonists from confronting each other, defusing situations as they occurred. We were lightly armed with our SLR rifles and some backup in the shape of a handful of Ferret scout cars armed with .50 calibre Browning machine guns, but that was it. If anything really serious had happened we would have had to just stand aside. Luckily it never came to that. We had a high regard for the Turkish army. Its soldiers were tough, smart, well disciplined and professional. The GCNG, on the other hand, were a bit of a shower. They lounged around their positions like disgruntled teenagers (which many probably were), bareheaded, smoking, and drinking coffee. Few of us were in any doubt that, if the Turks had decided to complete their conquest of the rest of the island, it would probably have taken them about twenty-four hours.

Most complaints from either side via the UN were petty in the extreme – a sandbag moved here, an encroachment into the buffer zone there – and were generally pathetic and pointless. Interestingly, the gunners (hawk, spit) we had taken over from had abandoned patrolling the buffer zone at night. I corrected this straight away and reinstated patrols round the clock, if for nothing else than a statement of intent and showing that we would not be pushovers by either side. We did, however, have a handful of incidents which were more substantial. Amongst these was the occasion when we were deployed to prevent a student demonstration crossing from the Greek side to the

Turkish side, a deliberate confrontation sought to highlight their half-hearted fight to reclaim homes lost during the ethnic cleansing of 1974.

Having grown up in the 1960s my image of a student demonstration was coloured by the riots in Paris in 1968 (when students and workers chanted 'le printemps sera chaud', amongst other things) and the waves of violence that had swept American campuses during protest there against the Vietnam War. I was somewhat surprised, therefore, to see groups of schoolchildren with their teachers turn out with placards to wave at the Turkish army and police. This was my first brush with school pupils being called students, an American affectation which increasingly pervades the UK media today.

Be that as it may, the Turks were clearly taking it seriously and had deployed heavily suited and booted riot police to meet any incursions. There were one or two minor surges towards the Turkish lines but they always stopped short, and having seen what was awaiting them I'm not surprised. I wouldn't have tackled the riot police either.

The other incident I recall was a blatant incursion into the Green Line by the Turkish side, where they unilaterally decided to shift their boundary towards the Greeks and did so, erecting signs announcing the fact. The local GCNG commander, a brigadier if I recall, asked me to go down and observe this outrage. I did so and found him 'up to high doh', threatening to carry out an attack to restore the integrity of the buffer zone.

This was pure bluff and bluster, because if he had carried out his threat it would have been both a serious international incident and a disaster for him and his men; they would have been swatted away like flies. But I had to do something. During a quick conflab with the CO he suggested I should deploy a troop to the area, stand out in front of them facing the Turkish lines, and see what happened. So we did, and lo and behold after about ten minutes the Turkish CO arrived and we had a quick parley through an interpreter he had brought along. At the end of our talk he basically said I should leave it to him, which I agreed. The next morning the encroachment, and the signs, were gone, removed during the night. We heard no more about it.

What did cause us the most hassle and heartache, though, was created internally, by my own soldiers. A couple of young troopers who obviously had an eye for the main chance had noted that security in Greek Cypriot shops was lax and that there were rich pickings to be had. They came up with a criminal *modus operandi* whereby the smaller of the two miscreants would conceal himself inside a shop just before closing time and get locked in. When the coast was clear he would then unlock from the inside and let his partner in, upon which they would then steal attractive items and be well clear when the shop re-opened in the morning.

What made their scheme doubly ingenious was that they did their stealing in southern (Greek) Cyprus but hid their stash in the UN buffer zone; the Greek Cypriot police had jurisdiction where the crimes were committed, but the UN Police had jurisdiction in the buffer zone, and there didn't appear to be any extradition agreement. So as long as they remained in the buffer zone they were untouchable by the Greek police. In fact we wouldn't have found out about their nefarious activities at all had it not been for the curiosity of Sergeant John Barnwell, who was intrigued by the fact that the Turks had started sending night-time patrols into the buffer zone, patrols which we confronted and sent back home. So he had a quick rummage around where the Turks had shown interest, discovered the stolen goods in a derelict building, and the game was up. The two thieves owned up when confronted with the evidence.

The problem was that they would be picked up by the Cypriot police if they left the buffer zone, and previous experience with such matters did not fill us with huge confidence in the Greek Cypriot justice system. The prospect of them rotting away in some nasty cockroach infested jail for years did not appeal to either them or us. So in the end we spirited them off the island. Charlie Pratt took them in his car to Limassol airport, bought their tickets on his credit card, and sent them back to Germany via the UK.

Naughty, I know, but we decided we had to look after our own. They were eventually court-martialled and dismissed from the army so justice was done in the end. Interestingly, the flight they were due to get on at the end of the tour was stopped and searched by the Greek Cypriot police on the runway at Larnaca, and they were understandably displeased that the two birds had flown. This particular case followed us all the way back to Germany, where the CO managed to sort it out.

These irritations and my general dislike for the tour aside, there were some attractions. Northern Cyprus had not then been ravaged by the tourism industry and was absolutely gorgeous, seemingly caught in a time warp from the 1950s. When in the UN we had free passage between the two parts of the island and made the most of it. I was particularly interested in some of the Crusader relics, including the mighty castle at St Hilarion in the mountains, and the port and harbour of Kyrenia was a favourite place for a simple meal and a drink as the sun went down.

There is much, much more that could be written about this particular UN tour but it'll have to wait for another opportunity. Suffice to say that I, and many others, were glad to see the back of the island after our 'sunshine posting'. We didn't know at the time that the Regiment would return for another tour only two years later, but this time I was not with them.

Chapter 15

Having heaved a huge sigh of relief on waving goodbye to Cyprus, it didn't take us long to get back into the swing of being an armoured regiment on tanks again. The rear party we had left behind whilst we were away had kept the panzers in pretty good nick in our absence and it wasn't long before we were back to normal once more. We were faced with a full training season: tactical training at the SLTA, live firing at Hohne Ranges, and then the ultimate confirmation of fitness for role at the BATUS in Alberta, Canada. But before all of that we had to go through all the low level training to get us back in tank mode after our six month holiday (sic) in Cyprus, and there seemed to be mountains of paperwork in the squadron office every day.

I had decided that I was a bit too old and stuffy to live with the younger bachelor officers in the mess anymore, so managed to swing moving to an empty MQ nearby, sharing with Richard Chesterfield, who was also old and stuffy but not quite to the same extent as me. It was a relief not to be the senior living-in officer anymore, and I'm sure it was a relief for the subbies that I had moved out too! With the best will in the world and no matter how relaxed I tried to be, I was always the senior older 'buftie' whose very presence constrained the youngsters from having fun on occasions, and it was much better for all of us if I was out of the way.

I remember little of annual firing at Hohne but it would have gone the way of all firing periods previously – individual tanks firing, then firing by troop, then firing on the move by troop, the latter called battle runs. One innovation that we did introduce, though, was the idea of firing and manoeuvring by half squadrons of seven tanks, one half commanded by me and the other by my 2ic Patrick Kidd. This was an attempt at the tactical level to bring more mass and firepower to the point of action than previously, and we continued the experiment throughout the year.

Then we went back to the familiar old Soltau for dry tactical training. That's dry as in no live ammunition, not as in alcohol free! The usual format ensued – troop training, squadron training, then 4 RTR BG training, for which we were joined by a couple of companies of the Royal Greenjackets, or 'the Jaikets' as the boys called them. They shared barracks with us in Osnabruck and were a pretty good outfit although we didn't socialise with them overmuch.

Soltau culminated with the brigade commander's test exercise which was a corker. The exact details of the activity escape me now, but I can remember being more exhausted at the end than at any other time in my army career, including Sandhurst. The exercise ended, as they always did, with the counterattack at dawn against the 'enemy', but I was so concerned that my tank crews would be so tired they wouldn't be awake when it was time to launch that I spent the entire night going from panzer to panzer making sure there was at least one crew member awake. I need not have worried, perhaps, because at dark o' clock in the morning when I gave the order to move they were all rolling straight away.

Then we went to Canada, flying Crab Air (RAF) via Keflavik in Iceland, which I discovered was a NATO base at the time. I have described the BATUS in a previous chapter, when I first went as a troop leader, so I won't reiterate the description again here. Suffice to say Camp Crowfoot was still the dusty and slightly scruffy camp in the middle of nowhere in Alberta. However, this time around, perhaps I was older and a bit more mature, I took better note of our surroundings.

The Canadian prairie was just as bleak and beautiful as I had found it on my first visit some seven or eight years previously. This time, however, I was much more sensitive to subtleties of the lay of the land and the colours of the landscape as the day progressed. The weather was perfect with glorious mornings and really hot days with blue skies all the time we were out, but the exercises were very demanding and we were exhausted by the end. My abiding memory is of the final counterattack my squadron was asked to carry out, and as we entered the valley where it was to happen I noticed a group of vehicles and individuals watching from a nearby hill. It turned out to be the corps commander, the divisional commander, and the brigade commander, all listening in to my squadron radio net as I gave the orders. Not much pressure there then!

We spent almost exactly a month in Canada, including seventeen days continuously out on the prairie living off our tanks. During this time we were almost oblivious to the deepening crisis in the Middle East following Saddam Hussein's occupation of Kuwait, although we knew that plans were afoot back in the UK and Germany. The training was hot, hard, and sometimes mind-numbingly exhausting, but on other occasions quite overwhelmingly exhilarating. At the end we felt we had acquitted ourselves well and were definitely fit for role.

On the second day of our return to the relatively civilised environment of Camp Crowfoot, a collection of prefabricated huts on the edge of the training area, the news reached us that 7th Armoured Brigade (7 Armd Bde) was being deployed to the Gulf. This was met with disappointment by some and relief by others; had 12 Armd Bde, which we were part of, been chosen, we ourselves would have been on our way.

The consensus amongst my colleagues was that we had no desire to be gassed or have our heads blown off on account of some mad tinpot dictator in an area of the world that held few attractions. Let others go, we said, and good luck to them. Little did we realise that back in Osnabruck the OC rear party had already been ordered to find 4 RTR personnel to augment 7 Armd Bde and that some of our younger officers were falling over themselves to volunteer. I discussed this phenomenon with one of my fellow squadron leaders at length and we agreed that being sent was one thing but volunteering was altogether another thing, and that both of us would wait for the former!

On return to Germany I gave up command of C Squadron and took up my new appointment of Regimental 2ic. I had been at my desk for only a morning and was still in the middle of taking over from my predecessor when, with no notice, the first batch of tradesmen from the REME descended on the regiment to strip our Chieftain tanks for spares for the Gulf. The CO, Charlie McBean, was not the sort of guy to take this sort of thing lying down but, after a couple of fairly heated phone calls, even he had to stand aside.

Thus, at a stroke, 4th Tanks was rendered non-operational and we were not to see our tanks whole again until long after the Gulf War was over. In the end, we provided amongst other things forty Chieftain gearboxes, thirteen engines, ten gun barrels and a host of other pieces of automotive and gunnery equipment. Our recce troop had engines and gearboxes stripped from all eight of its Scorpion CVR(T) vehicles. Particularly galling for the crews who had nurtured and maintained their tanks with pride over the years was the hasty and unprofessional way in which some of the stripping was carried out. In some cases the REME were found to have cut expensive cabling to remove items to save time and trouble unscrewing them. When the scavengers finally left we had not one of our fifty-seven tanks serviceable.

From this point onward, really, we became nothing more than an Op Granby (as the British operation had now been christened) support regiment. Over the next few months we provided assistance in many forms; we despatched paint teams to 7 Armd Bde units to help them prepare their vehicles; we lent our NBC instructors to help train deploying personnel in the face of the very real threat of the Iraqis using chemical and biological weapons; and we also had to supply a number of soldiers as battle casualty replacements (BCRs), to be held in reserve in the theatre of operations ready to be sent forward to replace those killed and wounded in action.

It all began to sound a bit serious, to be honest, and for me personally it got a whole lot more serious when I found myself nominated to go out and join our troops in the desert.

Chapter 16

So by late 1990 4th Tanks was an Op Granby support regiment, with our tanks stripped for spares to support the troops in the Gulf and increasing numbers of personnel being told off for other duties outwith the normal functions of a tank regiment. After my relatively short time as C Squadron leader I was now firmly ensconced as Regimental 2ic, nominally in charge of training – there wasn't any – and equipment – it had all been rendered useless. But there still seemed to be stacks going on.

Part of my new job was to publish the regimental forecast of events, a document that got updated from time to time and distributed to keep everybody up to speed with what was happening. It very quickly became an impossible task and we just started living day to day. Things changed constantly, much in line with the old army adages 'greatcoats off, greatcoats on' and 'rush to wait'. There is another, less complimentary army adage which describes the circumstances, and that is a 'cake and arse party'.

At this point I should probably say that I have written about this particular time in great detail in my short book *Sending My Laundry Forward: A Staff Officer's Account of the First Gulf War* (Troubadour, 2012, ISBN 978 1783064 182) and encourage you to go out and buy a copy. Except that you can't, because it's out of print. Actually, not quite true, I've just checked on Amazon and you *can* buy a new copy for £600. I would advise against this – it's not worth it, believe me. I am honour bound to say, therefore, that a lot of what follows hereafter is me plagiarising myself, shamelessly, from my last remaining copy of my book. (I thought you can't plagiarise yourself, by the way, but my better educated children tell me otherwise. Who knew? Well, apart from them obviously.)

Where was I? Oh, yes, the 'cake and arse party'. So, in the autumn of 1990, the Regiment's tanks were all VOR (vehicle off the road), the subbies were pleading with anyone who would listen to be allowed to volunteer to go to war (although interestingly not the NCOs, with one or two noticeable exceptions), the boys were being sent hither and thither to provide manpower for various tasks, and anything we planned came to nought. At this point I engaged my famous and immaculate sense of perfect timing and went on leave to get married, leaving chaos behind.

My honeymoon was spent exploring the farthest flung expanses of that great unexplored wilderness known as Devon, and on my way back I made the fatal mistake of popping into RHQ RTR in Dorset. I think I had to pick up something to take back to Germany, but, be that as it may, it was there that I heard for the first time that I might be bound for the Middle East. I think the deliverer of the information, the Regimental Colonel John Woodward, was disappointed that I did not appear more pleased, but bearing in mind I had been married a mere three weeks earlier I think my lack of enthusiasm was quite understandable.

There was to be no escape. On my return to Germany I continued with my new job as if nothing had happened. However, the rumours of my imminent departure for sunnier climes grew and grew, and eventually at one of the interminable conferences we held to try to bring some order to the madness the CO's phone rang. He answered, nodded and said 'Yes', then hung up. Turning to me he said 'That's you off then', or something like that. I was given a few days' leave to sort myself out personally and also to draw some new kit – respirator, NBC suit, 9 mm pistol etc – and that was that. I phoned my parents to tell them I was going. They were very philosophical about it.

Thus it came to pass, as they say in the Bible, that a few short weeks later I found myself bound for Saudi Arabia. Typically, when the army wanted you to go anywhere it chose the most inconvenient time for you to travel, and I left by car for the airport at the grisly time of 3.30 am. It was always the RAF's fault for they habitually insisted on early arrival at the point of departure and then kept us waiting around inconsiderately. We all hated the RAF transport system and personnel with a vengeance. Have I said this before? You can be sure I'll say it again before I'm done.

Also typically, this time of RHQ RTR, I had been told I was to join the Headquarters British Forces Middle East (HQBFME) in Jeddah. Unfortunately it wasn't there, it was in Riyadh. How on earth could they have got that so wrong? Thankfully Riyadh was where my plane was going, and I was in it together with lots of other poor souls on their way to war. Our journey was cheered up somewhat by the magician Paul Daniels, who was on his way out to visit the troops. He was actually brilliantly amusing and, unlike some of the senior officers in the forward 'business class' end of the plane, at least took the time to come back and chat to we mere mortals in economy.

I found myself in Egypt for the first and – so far – last time in my life when we landed to refuel in Cairo. My Dad had been in Cairo at various times during his time in the HLI in Palestine in 1946-48, and I was amused that I was in some small way following in his footsteps. We didn't deplane, though, just filled up with fuel in the middle of the night and then took off again. Thereafter it was a relatively short hop to Riyadh – or Riyadh, Saudi Arabia, as the Americans would say. It has always seemed to me the geography teaching in their high schools leaves something to be desired, but I suppose there will be another Riyadh somewhere in the USA so maybe it's fair enough.

Arriving at HQBFME was a bit of a Staff College reunion. I was picked up at the airport by Ian Rodley (RTR) and Richard Aubrey-Fletcher (Grenadier Guards), both of whom had been on the same course as I had. There were more when we got to the somewhat shabby and rundown office accommodation on an ordinary street which was to be our initial location. Friends and relatives had assumed we'd be in some bomb-proof underground bunker somewhere, but the only protection the building had was a guard company from the splendid Queen's Own Highlanders (QOHldrs) and a few sandbags round the entrance which we put up ourselves later.

The veterans of this organisation had themselves only been there for a matter of weeks. One of the first tasks of the earlier birds had been to go out to local stores and purchase their own desks, chairs, filing cabinets, and other bits of sundry office equipment, and then put them together so the place could operate. The money came from a seemingly bottomless treasure chest under the control of the QM. We now know that most of it was provided by the Saudi and Kuwaiti governments, and they were unstinting in their financial profligacy. Hardly surprising, I suppose, with the enemy at the gates of Saudi Arabia and in occupation of Kuwait as they were.

What did surprise me was that we were all housed in the Marriott Hotel. The reason was that the RAF was lead service for this particular little jaunt in the sand, initially at least, and they as an institution have never been known to settle for a four star hotel when there is a five star establishment available within a couple of hundred miles. So the Marriot it was. Had the RN been lead service I dare say we would have been billeted in some rusty, leaking hulk off the coast in the Gulf, and had it been the army we would doubtless have inhabited some vast, soulless tented camp in the middle of the desert, miles from any solace or entertainment. For reasons I have never fully understood we army boys like to make our lives as difficult as possible, an inherited masochistic tendency from many years before.

The fact that we were in a hotel did rather piss off the boys who were up country living off the back decks of their panzers, but what *really* hacked them off, and rightly so, was that we base-wallahs also got paid vast allowances for subsistence until the proper service catering services arrived and were set up. Our accommodation was free, and on top of our normal military salaries we were paid an additional £41 per day for food (1990 prices, equal to £85.29 today according to Google). And

My grandfather, Charles Crawford RAMC.

My uncle, Tom Crawford RA. Died from
illness on 9 July 1944 in Kent.

My father, Robert Crawford HLI.

4RTR tank park, Munster. (Photo: author)

Lieutenant Alan Dunlop and crew, Munster. (Photo: author)

Chieftain tanks on Hohne ranges. (Photo: unknown)

Me in my tank on the Rattlesnake Road, BATUS. (Photo: Bill Ashton)

Command troop, Munster. (Photo: author)

Me and Sergeant Peter Reid, Soltau training area, Germany. (Photo: Mark Outhwaite)

A typical 'smoker' in the field. (Photo: Niall Macnaughton)

4RTR Officers' Mess, Tidworth, May 1983 (Photo: unknown)

Pipe Major Harden BEM and Chieftain tank, Tidworth. (Photo: author)

Author firing AK47, Pakistan, 1983. (Photo: unknown)

Polo match with the Chitral Scouts, Swat Valley, Pakistan 1983 (Photo: author)

Staff College, Camberley, European tour, 1986 (Photo: author)

My cottage in Moreton, Dorset (Photo: author)

T E Lawrence's grave, Moreton churchyard (Photo: author)

Officers' mess, Dhekalia, 1989. (Photo: author)

Turkish trenches on the Green Line, Cyprus. (Photo: author)

UN Medal Parade, 29 September 1989. Author leading C Squadron with General Milner (Canada) taking the salute. (Photo: unknown)

My tank in BATUS, Canada, 1989. (Photo: author)

Replen in squadron leaguer, BATUS. (Photo: author)

Minor problem during a night march but nobody hurt, BATUS. (Photo: author)

Me at Al Jubail airstrip, Saudi Arabia, during the Gulf War 1991. (Photo: unknown)

Exhausted soldiers of the Queen's Own
Highlanders in a C130 Hercules aircraft,
Gulf War. (Photo: author)

The Highway of Death: Kuwait to Basra highway, Gulf War.
(Photo: author)

Me on post Gulf War leave in Switzerland. (Photo: author)

My house in Leavenworth, Kansas, while I was at the USACGSC 1992-93. (Photo: author)

Tropical service dress, Kansas. (Photo: author)

Me when SO1 (Image) at Army Headquarters Scotland. (Photo: Army HQ Scotland)

Out campaigning for the Scottish Parliamentary elections, 1999, in Roxburgh & Berwickshire. (Photo: unknown)

Cartoon that appeared in the Scottish press during the Scottish Parliamentary elections campaign, early 1999. (Artist: Steve Bright)

Arras Luncheon
Army and Navy Club, London
21 May 2021

MacNaughton ~ Miller ~ Polin ~Outhwaite ~ Eccles ~ Heyman ~ Horeau ~ Crawford ~ McGregor-Smith ~ Maunsell ~ Roberts
Gould ~ Large ~ Willis ~ Stephenson ~ Van-Berckel ~ Vaux ~ Lawson ~ Brown ~ Craven-Griffiths ~ Corbin
Turner ~ Whitfield ~ Goodson ~ Rose ~ Galloway ~ Cheshire
Vane-Percy

4RTR Exiles officers at the Arras Lunch, Army & Navy Club, 21 May 2021. (Photo: Simon Corbin, embellishments by Alex Finlay)

as we were dining mainly at the Wendy's Burger restaurant near the HQ there was no conceivable way of spending it.

It was a gravy train, and no mistake. By the time I arrived a little ritual had been established which I was advised to follow (and did). I drew my first batch of allowances – £540 if I remember correctly – from the paymaster's office and then went directly across the yard to the British Forces Post Office (BFPO) in the next portacabin, where I deposited the bulk of my money in a Post Office Investment Account. By the time these outrageous allowances were stopped most of us had amassed considerable savings in our accounts.

This theme of largesse continued when I went to pick up my staff car the next day, a brand spanking new Mazda 929 with twenty-three miles on the clock, courtesy of the Saudi government. It all felt a bit unreal, to be honest, and didn't last forever, but everybody made the most of it at the time. It was such a contrast to the usual mealy-mouthed stinginess that we were used to, and in many ways made us feel a bit more valued.

On my first working day at HQBFME I reported on arrival to the Chief of Staff (COS), Colonel Ian Talbot. He had no idea whatsoever that I was joining his staff and told me not to bother unpacking as he thought I should join 1 (UK) Armoured Division (1(UK) Div) in the field up country. Two hours later he changed his mind and told me I was staying. This set the pattern for the rest of my war (see 'cake and arse party' in the previous chapter). There was an early lesson here; don't believe that anyone else really knows what they're doing, they could be, and often were, bluffers. No criticism of Colonel Ian intended here, by the way, the situation was still, how might I put it, dynamic.

The first few weeks in theatre proved to be a bit of a 'sitzkrieg' or phoney war as the coalition forces built up in theatre and moved from the ports of entry inland. The logistical effort was staggering. At this point, being 'weapons trained' – that is trained in the design and acquisition of weaponry – I joined Lieutenant Colonel James Short, of the 9th/12th Lancers (9/12 L) I think, who had the unenviable task of dealing with all the multifarious demands for new equipment being made.

The fact that the Saudis and Kuwaitis were paying allowed every Tom, Dick and Harry to exercise their personal equipment aspirations and hobby-horses and requests for 'vital' kit were never-ending. It amused me that we had been ready to take on the massed Soviet tank armies with our kit as it stood, but now that we were facing the third world force that was the Iraqi army everything had to be up-armoured and enhanced. Nowadays I think they call it upgrading the vehicles to 'theatre entry standard', which can bring the weight of a modern Challenger 2 tank up to seventy-five tonnes, but the question remains the same: why isn't our equipment ready to go as it is?

Some of the more arcane equipment that I was involved in procuring included knobby tyres for motorcycles, to give them more traction in the sand, and smoke artillery rounds for our 155 mm artillery pieces. The only country that could supply the latter was South Africa, which at the time was still an international pariah because of apartheid, but it didn't seem to stop us buying ammunition from them. As it happened the war was over before the smoke rounds arrived.

So much kit was sent to the Gulf that we lost track of much of it. There was no asset tracking system in place as far as I'm aware and stuff got misplaced. Some of the containers sent from the UK were never opened at all, and the units up country got so fed up waiting for their bits and pieces that they sent people back to find what they needed, which only added to the confusion. More awkwardly, we lost a consignment of the then top secret Chobham armour for about forty-eight hours, a panic which ended when it was discovered on the edge of some airstrip somewhere and immediately put under close guard. If only the logistics staff had been able to barcode everything we'd probably have been all right, but they weren't able to do so.

During this time when the coalition forces were building up in theatre there were three main bones of contention which sowed dissent and envy amongst the troops, I'm afraid to say. The aforementioned expenses paid to us 'rear area oxygen thieves' (aka REMFs, which I will not expand upon in a family-friendly book) ranks first and foremost of these. Details have already been noted above, but their generosity bordered on the ludicrous, and we only got them thanks to the RAF's innate ability to screw every situation to their own advantage to the nth degree. They didn't last long, but the boys in the desert were peeved by them, put it that way, and rightly so. The BFPO outside in the yard was handling £250,000 per week as we all banked our allowances which gives some indication of the sums involved.

Next was the allocation of cars within HQBFME. As I wrote previously, I picked up a brand new Mazda 929 with twenty-three miles on the clock when I arrived, and most folk would have been quite satisfied with that. However, more senior officers were forever bickering over what level of car they should be entitled to. On one famous occasion I borrowed a Landrover Discovery to visit divisional HQ in the desert, and when I returned there just happened to be a *wheen* of senior officers in the car park who immediately demanded to know how I was entitled to that particular motor, and then proceeded to berate their junior staff officers as to why they didn't have one as well. It was truly pathetic.

But the biggest furore of all was over the issue of desert combat uniforms. The boys of 7 Armd Bde had managed to get themselves kitted out in desert appropriate clothing, with sand camouflage combats, desert boots, shemaghs and the like. They even got the rare sand woolly pully which was the mark of the *ancien combattant* and the object of envy for many Johnny-come-latelies like me. But then supplies ran out, and the rest of us turned up in our temperate green and brown combat kit which marked us out as the new boys in town. The issue of the next batches of desert combats became an issue – or not an issue (see what I did there?). So when the Chief of the General Staff (CGS), General Sir John Chapple, came out to visit us as he absolutely should have done, some idiot on his staff decided it would be a good idea to kit him and his entourage out in brand, spanking new desert combats whilst the troops in the field had none. I swear it looked as if his aide-de-camp (ADC) had ironed the general's outfit too, which added insult to injury. It was a PR *faux pas par excellence.*

However, the murmurings of discontent from the ranks were somewhat alleviated when the Deputy Chief of Staff (DCOS) of HQBFME, a colonel in the Royal Logistic Corps (RLC) who was responsible, amongst a myriad of more important items, for the distribution of said desert combats, declared that he would be the last man in theatre to get a set. He was true to his word and was the last British soldier dressed in green in theatre. We were impressed. He reminded me terribly of the comedian Ronnie Corbett and was a thoroughly decent chap.

With such things the tail end of 1990 passed slowly and soon we found ourselves in the Festive Season but a long way from home. After getting over our outrage that the Permanent Joint Headquarters (PJHQ) back at Northwood in the UK had gone on to skeleton manning for the period ('Skeleton manning? Don't they realise a war is about to begin?'), we were invited by British diplomats to spend Christmas Day with them in the diplomatic quarter in Riyadh, which was most kind of them. Many of them had managed to get out of Kuwait just in the nick of time.

It was as jolly as could be in the circumstances, and they had even got some Christmas presents for us, which was very touching. And, given diplomatic privileges, they could serve alcohol too, which we had been more or less deprived of since we arrived in Saudi. Of course it went straight to our heads and we became *unco' fu'*. However we drove home afterwards nonetheless, reasoning that a state which banned alcohol would have no need for drink driving laws and therefore we were quite safe from prosecution. And the driver went on to become a brigadier in later life!

We did get sent alcohol from back home, of course, despite many warnings that we were breaking Saudi law. At first it came surreptitiously, disguised in shampoo bottles and marked accordingly on the customs forms. Trouble was that the WAGs who sent it never rinsed out the containers well enough, and thus the Glenmorangie so transported tasted like Head 'n' Shoulders. Then someone brazenly sent me some marked 'whisky' on the package and it arrived safely and without mishap. After that we were all much more relaxed, both mentally and physically. Lots of us had lost our taste for it, though, so there was little over-indulgence that I knew of in HQBFME.

The other great advantage we had over the boys in the desert was a facility we called Freefone Saudi Arabia. Basically the phones in the HQ had no barriers to private use and were open to international calling. During the nightshift, in particular, there were long hours of boredom which could be pleasantly alleviated by calls to friends and family back home. We spent quite literally hours talking to friends and relatives, all courtesy of the Saudi government. Word got out, and our chums in the field would call us on the military net and ask us to call up their WAGs to tell them that they were, so far at least, safe. We were of course happy to oblige.

And that was about it. The new year of 1991 arrived and we found ourselves many miles from home without any real clue what was coming next. That, however, was all about to change.

Chapter 17

Nineteen ninety-one found all of us at HQBFME in reasonably good spirits. By now we realised that the chances of resolving the crisis in the Gulf without going to war were slipping away. With nearly 430,000 US troops in Kuwait Theatre of Operations (KTO) and Saddam Hussein threatening to attack Israel, it seemed that there was little room for diplomatic manoeuvre left.

Actually 1991 was nearly a very short year for me. Travelling down the motorway on one of our visits to Div HQ in the desert we had a blow out in our car at 100 mph. We were going at what some might consider to have been excessive speed but the road was wide and new, so we thought nothing of it. The burst tyre led to much screeching and swerving (the car that is, not us) and it was exciting at the time but the driver, a civvy called Chris Coomber, managed to keep control. We were aided by the fact there was no other traffic on the road. It certainly got the heartbeat up a bit but otherwise we were OK. A quick change of wheel, a dust down, and we were again on our way.

The desert was ... pink! Did you know that? I always thought it was a sandy colour but the bit I saw was definitely pink. Which might explain why the SAS, who are well hard and not generally associated with girly colours, tend to paint their vehicles accordingly when involved in desert ops. Who knew? I didn't, but now I've seen it with mine own eyes I understand. Later on I discovered that the RAF had painted their Tornados and Jaguars pink too, so I wasn't imagining it.

But I digress. The desert was absolutely covered with military kit. As far as the eye could see there were vehicles static and moving, tented camps, supply dumps and all the other paraphernalia that signifies a major military operation. It took some time to locate Div HQ as signposting wasn't a major success and one tented location under a camouflage net looked just like the others. I found it eventually, but it was in the middle of an NBC exercise and everybody was masked up and in their noddy suits. I put my stuff on to conform, but verbal communication was nigh on impossible. It was farcical to be honest. I couldn't even see who I was talking to; it could have been the general and I'd have been none the wiser.

When the exercise ended and we all got back to normal I did my rounds of the various desks to ask what people needed. At the end of the day I went for dinner in the HQ mess tent, noting with much amusement that the guards on duty had already all gone a bit native and were dressed in a combination of British temperate and desert combats, bits of American kit they had swapped, and the bright pink Saudi shemaghs that the locals favoured. Nobody paid a blind bit of notice, perhaps because historically the British army has always seemed to go a bit T.E. Lawrence in the desert.

After an uncomfortable night in some temporary hut, sharing with a sergeant-major who complained bitterly that 'he hadn't joined up for this sort of thing', I made my way back to

Riyadh. Stopping for petrol on the way back I was conscious of a small boy watching my every move, probably because I was wearing my pistol as we did at all times. At that time, and maybe it also applies now, I thought it the most soulless city I had ever visited. It was as if vast wealth had suddenly come to a backward and mediaeval people and they had decided to spend it all on their idea of American culture. Oh, hang on a minute …

Back at HQBFME our spirits were hardly lifted by a visit by the Prime Minister, John Major, of whom some of you may have heard previously. If you haven't don't worry because you haven't missed anything. He came and gave a little morale-shattering (boosting, surely?) speech to the staff, but I couldn't be bothered going next door to listen to a stream of well-intentioned but mindless platitudes, and so I caught up with my paperwork instead. To be fair, nowadays it could have been Boris Johnson visiting, so we must be thankful for small mercies.

On 12 January 1991 we went on to twenty-four hour manning and I was designated to join the nightshift on the Land Cell operations desk. Things became noticeably more serious at this point; the Americans started wearing helmets and body armour and our guards from the QOHldrs became doubly vigilant. Worst news for many was that, there now being sufficient number of us in HQBFME, we now qualified for a catering unit and therefore subsistence allowances were to stop. The gravy train thus came to an end.

I shared the nightshift with Richard Aubrey-Fletcher and Henry Spender, both nice chaps, and we all got on well. Generally speaking there was much less to do at night although we were to have some excitement in the weeks ahead. Working through the wee small hours was a bit strange to begin with, and we all found it extremely difficult to stay awake initially. However, after a few nights our body clocks adjusted and we were fine. Just as well, for we were to be on constant nightshift for a couple of months.

Much of our time began to be taken up answering some rather basic detailed questions from PJHQ at High Wycombe back in the UK, the pettiness of which began to irritate us. It was, in retrospect, a sign of how little they had to do and how left out of the picture they sometimes felt. We tried to explain that there wasn't actually all that much going on in Saudi Arabia, but they never quite believed us and always thought we were hiding something. I was taken to task once for not reporting the discovery of a hand held rocket launcher on the beach, such was their thirst for information, any information. 'Did it mean that Iraqi special forces had landed behind our lines', they asked? 'Did it Hell' I replied, probably one of our allies had forgotten about it after a swim.

It was clear though that time for a peaceful solution was running out fast. We got to the point where the Iraqis couldn't actually get out of Kuwait within the parameters set by the UN resolution even if they'd wanted to. I was still unaware of any plan to oust the Iraqis from Kuwait but I guessed that some of my colleagues were better informed than I. It didn't take the brains of an archbishop to work out that any operation would probably start with some sort of air attack, but that's as much as I had thought about it. We all knew it was coming soon though.

The night shift reported for work at 9.30 pm in the evening of 16 January and we were instantly aware that something was going on. Nothing was said, nor was there anything out of the ordinary happening, but we could feel that the atmosphere was quite different. There was something intangible about the place, an unspoken anticipation that set us all on edge. We went for 'lunch' at midnight as usual, a meal taken outside the HQ in a lean-to shed in the back yard where the RAF cooks produced standard forces fare which had come as a welcome relief after our first few weeks' existence on Wendy Burgers and little else.

As we munched on our sausage and chips I was aware that there was a seemingly endless succession of aircraft taking off from the airport nearby. I mentioned this to Richard A-F, who looked at me in a funny way and said that he thought that maybe 'something was going on'. At that point I knew that he knew, and that I was about to find out. Sure enough, I was back at the Land Cell Ops desk at 1.50 am when the Assistant Chief of Staff Ops (ACOS Ops) announced that US forces had just launched 100 cruise missiles at Iraq. We were briefed formally at 02.00 am that hostilities against Iraq had commenced. At long last the air war had started.

As it turned out, although we were being briefed just as the first raids were starting, we learned that US special forces had gone into action some time earlier to neutralise some Iraqi radars thereby allowing coalition aircraft to cross the border undetected. Suddenly aware that it was all happening, we turned to the television with a kind of awful fascination to confirm what we had just been told. CNN was broadcasting live from Baghdad and we were treated to the mother of all fireworks shows as every Iraqi gun blasted blindly into the night air, not being able to detect the US F117A stealth fighters that were bombing their city. Back in Riyadh we then embarked on a series of air raid and NBC warnings which had us struggling in and out of our NBC suits. Nothing actually came our way that night, of course, but it did add to the excitement of the occasion!

So the air war had finally started. We rapidly became swamped with information and statistics – so many radars destroyed there, so many aircraft hit by small arms fire, so many sorties over Baghdad. Very little of it was verifiable or attributable, and we fielded non-stop calls from the UK which were just irritating; how many bombs have the RAF dropped? How many US aircraft have been lost? The truth was we didn't have a bloody clue most of the time.

It wasn't too long before the Iraqis fired back. On the second night of the air war we had great excitement. At about 3.00 am we were notified of an Iraqi missile launch against Israel. This in many ways was the nightmare scenario because if Israel responded there was a fear that the Coalition might not survive. We thought our Arab allies unlikely to support an attack by their traditional enemy on one of their own, albeit an unpopular and ostracised one. After much scurrying to and fro and frantic phone calls from the UK, we established that eight missiles had been launched in all; three landed in Tel Aviv, two in Haifa, two dropped short in Iraq and one was never accounted for or confirmed.

These missile attacks had two fairly dramatic results. The first was that in the HQ we got reports that there might be some evidence of nerve agent at the points of impact. This got us understandably twitchy (the news, not the nerve agent). Our

NBC officer was a relatively junior captain, but on his shoulders now fell the decision whether or not we should start taking our prophylactic medicine against nerve agent poisoning, called the Nerve Agent Pre-Treatment Set (NAPS). With no time to refer to a higher authority he quite rightly decided that we should start taking our tablets straight away. The decision was passed down to all 43,000 men and women of the British contingent who also started on the treatment.

Meanwhile Israel had scrambled approximately seventy-six combat and supporting aircraft to strike back immediately and, unbelievably we thought, seemed to have secured agreement to transit Syrian airspace to reach Iraq. The Coalition and Israel then came to a speedy arrangement over deconfliction of airspace over Iraq, and a line was drawn down the chart in our Ops Room to show the demarcation. It really did seem as if things were going to escalate in a major way. Thankfully wiser counsel prevailed and the Israelis never carried through with their attack, but it was a close run thing for a moment or two.

The fourth night of the air war, that of 20/21 January, was to be the most dramatic to date as far as we on the night shift were concerned. As we arrived in the Ops Room three SCUD missiles were fired by the Iraqis at Dhahran, the main US port for disembarkation in Saudi Arabia, and there were a few tense moments until we heard the US had fired five of its Patriot missiles to intercept and that they claimed all the incoming missiles had been destroyed. (We were later told informally that the Patriot missile system had a claimed kill rate of circa seventy per cent, but in fact it was probably closer to seventeen per cent!)

All went quiet again until we went for our lunch at midnight, taken as usual in the lean-to shack in the back yard of the HQ. Word came of another missile alert as we were savouring our sausage and chips (did we have anything other than sausage and chips? I can't remember now), and then a cheerful clerk opened the back door of the main building and told us that this time Riyadh was the target. Quickly we scrambled into our noddy suits on the spot as our food went cold, and then were treated to the sight of three or four Patriot missiles being launched to intercept by the US battery just up the road at the airport.

These bad boys went off and quickly broke through the sound barrier with resultant sonic booms and then disappeared into the clouds. It was a bit like Guy Fawkes night for a moment, and then we remembered that these SCUDs could possibly have had chemical warheads so we masked up quickly. At this point Richard A-F and I decided that our proper place was in the ops room so we abandoned our sausage 'n' chips and ran down the street towards the main entrance.

As we did so, it appeared that an incoming missile was intercepted and detonated directly over our heads – or so it seemed – with a quite thunderous roar and flash of red. It was a bit like being caught in the middle of a severe thunderstorm, except the lightning flashes were bright pink. I remember quite distinctly that the dust in the street bounced at the point of detonation. Awesome.

It became clear later on that the US missile expenditure that first night had been enormously profligate and extravagant; thirty-five Patriots had been fired to intercept just six SCUDs launched at Riyadh by the bad guys. Command and control of the Patriot units was apparently the problem. There were three batteries of them around Riyadh at this stage in the proceedings, but they were not yet controlled centrally. The Patriot system was apparently designed to launch two missiles at each incoming unfriendly missile to ensure a kill. Each of the three batteries tracked the six SCUDs, and as there was no central fire control system yet set up, each fired twelve missiles (one misfire) at all six SCUDs.

The end result was a firework display which easily surpassed the annual firework concert display at Edinburgh Castle during the Festival, and which no doubt eventually presented the Saudi government with a bill far in excess of that justified by the actual threat. According to the Washington Post, 'A total of 158 missiles, which cost an estimated $1 million each, were used to intercept the 47 rudimentary SCUD missiles launched by Iraqi military' during the course of the war. Not all were targeted on Saudi Arabia of course, with an estimated twenty-four Iraqi SCUDs aimed at Israeli cities. But I'm getting ahead of myself …

Funnily enough, this first raid on Riyadh gave a major boost to those of us working in HQBFME. We all had been a little bit ashamed of our cushy lifestyle whilst the boys roughed it out in the desert. Now, however, we had been the first to come under attack and, despite the lack of any real danger, we could at least claim that we had been fired at in anger. It may have gone some small way to defuse some of the understandable resentment that the front line troops felt. I am reliably informed that when the news of the missile attacks on Riyadh reached them they all cheered.

For my part I lost no time in sending a signal back to 4 RTR in Germany claiming to be the first member of the regiment to have come under fire in the current conflict, if indeed not since Korea. The message was sent with my tongue firmly in my cheek and would have been treated with the expected good humoured derision when received. We did feel, however, that we were now really at war and that the conflict was no longer something that we were just seeing on CNN.

The following days and nights continued in a similar vein. I got caught out again, this time on my own out in the car, collecting a few personal things I had left in the wrong place. As I drove back to the HQ the air raid sirens started up again. All Hell was let loose on the roads as Saudi drivers, never the most competent or predictable at the best of times, went into a collective blind panic. Ignoring all the road signs and traffic lights – not to mention the speed limits – they drove at breakneck speed with horns blaring in their unseemly haste to get home or to the nearest shelter. In any other circumstances it would have been mildly amusing, but at the time it was all just a bit pathetic.

Later I calculated that up to that point the Iraqis (pronounced 'Eye-rack-ees' by the way, with a south of Mason – Dixon Line twang if you're a Gulf vet) had fired thirty-one SCUD missiles and had killed one person; as a military weapon in Iraqi hands the SCUD had proved to be pretty poor, but they had considerable political impact and an ever increasing amount of time and effort was being committed to hunt them down. Their launches were picked up immediately by US satellites because of their firing signature, and the Hereford Hooligans (aka SAS) were already deep inside Iraq trying to find them. But still they came.

Coalition air forces flew day and night to try to track down and destroy the mobile launchers that the Iraqis used to launch their attacks, and SAS patrols were inserted deep inside Iraq to try to do the same, but they were mainly unsuccessful. The Iraqis hid the launchers in culverts and under highway bridges, and it took only half an hour to deploy and launch before they scurried away to their hiding places again. Of the approximately 100 missile launchers claimed as destroyed by Coalition air and special forces during the course of the war, not a single claim could be verified afterwards. Indeed, post war, investigations showed that the Iraqis still had twenty or so launchers and sixty-two missiles intact.

Chapter 18

The air war had a way to run yet and raged on. Back at our superior HQ in the UK they were beginning to get a bit twitchy at the number of Tornados the RAF was losing – five in combat and one to a malfunction so far. We all knew that something was wrong somewhere, for the USAF was flying four or five times as many sorties but were losing barely twice the number of aircraft. Mind you, the Tornado JP233 airfield denial munition which was the Tornados' weapon of choice at this point required them to fly straight and level down the middle of the Iraqi runways at about fifty feet. All the bad guys had to do was lie on their backs at either end of the runway and fire up in the air; they were bound to hit something.

By 23 January the Coalition had flown approximately 10,000 sorties, and whilst battle damage assessment (BDA) was still sketchy, we knew that it must be having some considerable effect, if only because the Iraqis seemed unable, or unwilling, to do anything about it. There was also some skirmishing on the Iraqi-Saudi border on the night of 22/23 January, with some Iraqi prisoners taken. On a lighter note, the British medical unit 32 Field Hospital was nearly captured intact as it drove up from Al Jubail, the British port of entry, to join the division in the middle of the night, missed the turning, and was only stopped just before it drove straight into Iraqi-occupied Kuwait. What a PR disaster that would have been!

Things settled down after the mayhem of the first few days of the air war, but we were mystified by the lack of Iraqi response. Their navy was being destroyed, their airfields, command and communication centres, and political/military/economic assets were being rapidly eroded, and their only serious air sortie had been shot out of the sky by Saudi F15s. On top of all this, the Iraqi army was being hammered in situ from the air, with one of their Republican Guard Force Divisions (RGFC) being bombed every half hour by US B52 bombers. There was now some speculation that the Coalition ground forces might not need to go into action at all given the success of the air campaign. The old debate about whether wars could be won by air power alone started all over again.

The SCUD raids continued but had lost some of their fear factor through familiarity and the fact that rarely was anyone hurt or anything damaged. An exception occurred on the night of 25/26 January when two missiles were fired at Riyadh. Four Patriot were launched to intercept, but there was still an extremely loud bang seemingly close to the HQ as at least one warhead landed. We were masked up for twenty minutes or so whilst investigations found out that some damage had been done to a nearby building and possibly one person had been killed and several injured. Later we were able to see television pictures of the remains of the missile lying in a street not too far away from us.

We now had developed a little routine for dealing with these attacks. The alarm came on our computer screens as soon as the US satellites picked up the launch signature. Non-essential personnel went quickly to the basement which offered a modicum of cover and stayed there until the all clear was sounded. Of those left, usually two of us on the Land Cell desk, one made all the required calls reporting the imminent attack to PJHQ in the UK, the division in the desert (which as previously reported usually led to loud cheering as we in the cushy rear were discomfited), and to various other organisations in theatre.

The other got into his NBC suit, and then the roles were swapped. This took roughly about four minutes, and as we knew by then that the average time which elapsed between the attack warning and the missile arriving was about eight minutes, we spent the remaining four minutes reading the newspapers, telling jokes, chatting, and watching the clock. It was always quite a relief when we heard the missile land or be intercepted and we knew we were unharmed, but eventually we became quite blasé about it. Even the local citizens had become notably more relaxed about these raids and were frequently seen scrambling on to the rooftops with video cameras to record the SCUDs' arrivals.

Around this time I received my second anthrax and whooping cough *jags*, plus one against bubonic plague which came as a bit of a surprise. There is no ceremony about getting inoculated in the army, folks. You just line up with everybody else and get them all at the same time, in both arms. As expected these made us all feel a bit ropey, although we did laugh when we heard that the senior medical officer responsible for administering the vaccinations had taken the following day off because he felt unwell! Personally, I would have dragged myself into work even if half dead to avoid the embarrassment; an example of leadership *a la* Sandhurst ethos it most definitely was not.

To our great delight we also became 'SCUD aces' when Riyadh was attacked for the fifth time. That particular night eight missiles in all were fired by the Iraqis, with six going to Israel, one towards the US base at Dhahran, and one at us. Damage in Riyadh was negligible. However, despite all the bombing the Iraqi army was still a force to be reckoned with, and the night of 29/30 January saw the first significant moves on the ground for some time. It began with reports from the US Marine Corps, more or less directly south of Kuwait City, of enemy tanks crossing the border. One of the incursions seemed to be heading straight down the coast road towards the Saudi coastal town of Ras Al Khafji.

The situation was extremely unclear for most of the night and all our attempts to get more detailed information were unsuccessful. Eventually we heard that the marines were claiming fifteen enemy tanks destroyed for the loss of two of their own light armoured vehicles (LAVs). Sadly one of the US AC 130 gunships which had been supporting the operation stayed around for too long after daybreak and was shot down, killing all its crew. Later the US Marines admitted their own casualties as eight to ten killed and about twenty wounded.

As February arrived things became noticeably quieter overall. There were still missile attacks by the Iraqis on both Saudi Arabia and Israel but we had become so blasé about them by this time that sometimes we forgot to mention them in our handover briefings to the incoming day shift. There had been some amusing moments during the raids; in one of them one of our fellow officers had scrambled down to the basement of our living accommodation dressed only in boxer shorts and gas mask. During the raid he fell asleep, and at the all clear was left there as a joke by his comrades. The poor chap woke some hours later, frozen, disorientated, and still wearing his gas mask, swearing terrible revenge on those who had left him behind.

On another occasion the same individual and a friend were out in a local restaurant for lunch during one of the rare daylight SCUD attacks. When the alarm sounded they assumed it was another false alarm – there were many – and continued with their meal, laughing at the antics of the waiters who had only one gas mask between them and were taking it in turns to breathe through it. They quickly stopped laughing when things started to go bang in the sky, and to their dismay found they had left their NBC kit and respirators in the car and couldn't get to them because the waiters had locked the restaurant door. Being gassed in a burger restaurant because you had forgotten to bring your NBC kit would not have been a particularly glorious way to appear on the casualty list. And he was a Guards officer too! The social shame would surely have been too much to bear.

Not surprisingly, with so little going on that affected us directly, life at the HQ became a little dull. On the night shift in particular there was very little to do. We all made the most of the spare time to write home, and I must have written to nearly everybody I could think of whose address I knew. I was also pleasantly surprised by the letters I received from friends of whom I had not heard for many years. I even got a couple of

phone calls from civilian friends while I sat at the ops desk –
how on earth they got the number I never found out.

Use of 'Freephone Saudi Arabia' was rife and rumours
were constantly circulating that the day of reckoning was fast
approaching. On one famous occasion a spoof bill for many
thousands of pounds was issued on official notepaper to one of
the most profligate culprits, sending him into a deep depression
until he was let off the hook. Oh how we laughed. In the end,
however, we all got away with it.

None of us were particularly enamoured with what little
we saw of Saudi social life. We had expected a male orientated
society for sure, but I don't think we were ready for the true
extent of it. The women were very much in the background, and
we seldom spoke to any. Funnily enough, when we bumped into
them without any Saudi men around, in the lift at the Marriott
for example, they were very quick to open the conversation, but
as soon as a Saudi male entered they were silent.

I used to watch the men socialising at night in the hotel, a
ritual which seemed to consist entirely of drinking coffee with
the male members of their families, and my immediate thought
was how sterile their social lives were. This, of course, was an
entirely ethnocentric judgement. I just couldn't understand
how they enjoyed themselves, that's all. A social life without
alcohol is easy and no barrier to fun, but the absence of female
company is another thing altogether.

Rumour had it that the women's custom of dressing
in black from head to foot and wearing a veil gave them
complete anonymity and allowed them to partake in all sorts of

indiscretions, but I doubt it very much. We referred to them as 'Guinness bottles' or MBOs – mobile black objects – which wouldn't be very woke nowadays. But I felt sorry for the women and, correspondingly, a degree of antipathy towards the Saudi male. As for the country as a whole, it felt to me as if a society of mainly simple peasant people had suddenly been granted riches beyond their wildest dreams in the space of a generation and was struggling to come to terms with it, which is of course more or less exactly what had happened.

Our morale got a fillip with the announcement that the Saudi government was going to give us all a medal, so all 43,000 British servicemen and women were going to have something to hang on our chests afterwards. We all hoped that the British government would also authorise a campaign medal, and wondered whether the Kuwaiti government would follow the Saudi lead too. (They did, but we weren't allowed to wear them. Spoilsports.) I think we had visions of returning with chestfuls of medals clanking as we marched in the victory parade down the Mall. In fact, the award of campaign medals became one of the more emotive issues in the war, right up there with the payment of allowances, the issue of desert combat uniform, and the aforementioned provision of hire cars.

All of us thought we were entitled to them having been in theatre and been fired at by 'the baddies', but we became quite irritated when we learned that, for example, those working at PJHQ in the UK considered themselves worthy recipients too. Where did one draw the line? In the end it was all sorted out amicably, but there were all sorts of anomalies. A celebrated, and possibly apocryphal, example was that those attending a polo course in Cyprus, which technically was within SCUD range, were to receive the Gulf medal despite having absolutely nothing to do with the campaign. I was pleased to hear that some COs had banned those who had 'won' their medals in this way from ever wearing them.

A couple of nights later the Americans dropped two 15,000 airburst bombs on the Iraqis, and we watched video footage of them being launched from the open cargo bays of a Hercules transport aircraft. For the first time I heard doubts expressed on the morality of our actions. It seemed to be an awful lot of death and destruction to visit on people who were essentially defenceless against air attack by this stage, and some of us didn't like it very much. We hoped that the US wasn't just using the war as a convenient testing ground for its weapons systems. It was interesting to see that, even in a war which most of us felt was justified, although we were generally cynical as to the *real* reason we were there, a strong sense of fair play remained. This feeling was to emerge again later in the war when the Iraqis were caught from the air on the Kuwait to Basra highway, the infamous Highway of Death.

Around this time I met Mark Urban, now the BBC Newsnight presenter, in Riyadh. He had served with 4 RTR back in the early 1980s and I knew him quite well, so we had lunch together at the Marriott. By this time I was fully *au fait* with the Coalition ground attack plan, which was of course secret, but naturally Mark sounded me out on what I thought would happen. I couldn't say anything, but by starting from first principles he already had an extremely accurate view of how the ground attack might unfold. For a start, he knew that

1 (UK) Div was not where we said it was but much further west. He had also assessed the terrain from which he correctly guessed it would lend itself perfectly to the division executing an armoured left hook into northern Kuwait, thereby cutting off and isolating the bulk of the Iraqi troops there. In fact he got most of it right, and in retrospect I'm surprised the enemy didn't second guess it too. After our short meeting Mark went up country and I didn't see him again during the campaign.

On 10 February the Foreign Secretary, Douglas Hurd, came round the HQ on a visit. I shook his hand and remember thinking how ill he looked. He was terribly nice, and I attempted to brief him off the large scale map on the current situation but without much success. It wasn't helped when he said something along the lines of 'So this is where the Division is', and pointed at a spot on the map about 500 kilometres off its actual location. To be fair, I reckon he had more than enough on his plate at that point and the precise location of our chaps was the least of his worries. At least he came round to say hello and broke up the general tedium at the time.

We did, however, now know the date of G Day, the day the Coalition ground offensive was due to start. John Cantwell, an Aussie on attachment to Div HQ and who claimed to have been specially 'licensed to die' by the Australian government so he could take part in the war, came down to Riyadh from the division. He was looking for any information we could give him on Iraqi dispositions in the path of the division's projected advance. Despite the Coalition's array of sophisticated surveillance and target acquisition systems and its ability to fly at will across Iraq, the troops in the front line had very little information on the enemy at the tactical level, it seemed.

The intelligence system was simply swamped by the vast amount of information being gathered from all sources and very little properly sifted intelligence filtered down to those at the sharp end. In particular, 1 (UK) Div wanted photographs of the Iraqi positions they would have to attack and I think we at HQBFME were able to get some for them. The Americans didn't seem to be capable of getting this sort of low-level information, although their strategic and operational stuff was remarkably good. Cantwell told us his task in the forthcoming operation and my reaction was that he was a goner and we wouldn't see him again on this Earth. Thankfully I was wrong. He made the most of his short stay in the Marriott with us and enjoyed his first bath for a month, following it up with several more one after the other until he felt fully clean.

On St Valentine's Day the news was dominated by the deaths of approximately 500 Iraqi civilians in a bunker in Baghdad, hit and destroyed by two bombs from an F 117 stealth fighter. The US authorities were adamant that it was a communications centre and therefore a legitimate target, but it was a terrible event and in the HQ we felt awful about it. For all the trumpeting there had been about the new generation of precision weapons and concomitant reduction in collateral damage, innocent civilians had still been killed and injured. We seemingly hadn't made much progress over the past fifty years.

There was also the suspicion that the RAF might have killed some Iraqi civilians on the same day during a bombing raid on bridges over the Tigris, and the media picked up this one too. Later we saw video footage taken by the attacking aircraft which confirmed our worst fears; at least a couple of bombs had failed to be guided properly to the intended target and had hit the village beyond it. We euphemise such events as collateral damage, but in the end it was ordinary civilians going about their everyday lives who would have been killed. How very sad.

Chapter 19

And then, all of a sudden, it was G Day. At 1.00 am GMT on 24 February 1991 it all started – the biggest land operation since the Normandy landings in 1944, so we were told. As is well recorded elsewhere, the Coalition attack on Iraq was phased, with different elements attacking at different times to catch the enemy unawares and deceive him as to where the main effort lay.

At H Hour, 4.00 am local time, the American XVIII Corps and the French 6 Armoured Division, on the Coalition's western flank, were first off the mark into Iraq and made remarkably quick progress. In the eastern part of the theatre, the US Marines attacked north into Kuwait and towards Kuwait City, and immediately had the strange and unforeseen experience of being hampered by crowds of surrendering Iraqi soldiers as soon as they breached the border berm. After about six hours they were some thirty kilometres into Kuwait and it appeared there was nothing left to stop them.

Even at this early stage in proceedings we began to wonder if it might be all over much faster than we had originally thought. We were really rather busy for the whole shift for once – briefing PJHQ on developments as best we could as communications with our division were poor – and looking to see if we could bring the schedule forward if the enemy was truly routed. Our COS, Colonel Ian Talbot, was buzzing around the HQ like a bluebottle on amphetamines and quickly became labelled as 'the rogue Patriot' for his behaviour, reminiscent of a missile which had lost its guidance. The pace was indeed frenetic, but soon settled down as we became used to working in a climate of constant change and imperfect knowledge. As the end of the first day of ground action arrived 1 (UK) Div was all set to go, just waiting for the US 1st Infantry Division – the Big Red One – to secure the breach in the border berm and minefields.

Our boss General Sir Peter de la Billiere got a briefing every morning, and the night shift presented it at 8.00 am so the day shift could be brought up to speed at the same time before taking over. I often marked up the main briefing map at about 6.30 am in preparation, and it was not unusual for the general to appear at that early hour from his nearby bunk, still in dressing gown and slippers with a mug of tea in his hand, to get an early informal update on what had happened overnight.

Such was the uncertainty and difficulty in getting accurate information from the boys in the desert that he sometimes left these early morning sessions none the wiser, for I recall that I often had to reply 'I don't know' to his questions. I'm sure he realised the difficulties we faced and was always understanding of our lack of detailed knowledge. We were usually a little bit better informed by the proper briefing at 8.00 am, but even then we never really got any information on the fortunes of our Arab allies apart from BBC and CNN news reports.

These formal briefings always followed the same format. The RAF watchkeepers spoke first with a weather forecast for the next twenty-four hours followed by a review of air operations over the last twenty-four hours. We were on next, with me briefing on the flow of Coalition operations in general then Richard Aubrey-Fletcher on the progress of 1 (UK) Div in detail. The RN came next, and then a host of others on supply, medical, prisoners of war, etc. It usually lasted about an hour and was videotaped throughout. I was struck once again by the similarity of the proceedings to a typical staff college exercise at Camberley, and it was sometimes hard not to regard the assembled audience as the DS from that institution who had come to assess and grade the performance. I rather enjoyed these briefings by the end, for I quickly realised that, whilst I actually knew very little of what was happening across the theatre of operations, most of the audience knew considerably less. In the land of the blind, as they say ...

The ground campaign made dramatic advances over the next few days, and I won't bore you with the detail of unit movements and clashes which have been well documented elsewhere. It was breathtaking in its scale and yet the enemy was failing to respond. Perhaps, rather like us, they were almost mesmerised by the drama as it unfolded and were somehow rendered unable to do anything about it, or perhaps it was the Coalition's mastery of the skies which kept the bulk of the Iraqi forces stationary and concealed as best they could manage.

Even at this early stage we became critical of our own success, and much ado began to be made of our division's relative immobility to date, having not yet moved through the breach which was to be delivered by the Americans. This theme was to resurface on a number of occasions later and I had to agree at the time that compared to our US allies we sometimes appeared pedestrian and lacklustre in our manoeuvres. But in this particular case it was solely because the US Big Red One division took rather longer than anticipated to move itself through the breach it had created in the border defences – such as they were. I fielded a number of agitated phone calls from PJHQ from people who rather irritatedly asked 'what was wrong with our division', and did my best to explain.

Such was the speed of progress overall, however, that Op Trebor, the HQBFME draft plan to move elements of our HQ to Kuwait itself as soon as was feasible, were soon being dusted off. We realised that we might in fact be back in Kuwait well before we had imagined. I must admit it was hard at this point to understand exactly what was going on in the desert. Our communications were temperamental, we were living in a luxurious hotel and driving to work like civilians, and we were in no real danger. For us the whole affair was always in danger of degenerating into a gigantic board game.

On 26 February the boys for the Kuwait operation were chosen, that is those who were to set up HQBFME (Forward) in the old British Embassy building in Kuwait City, and with a mixture of disappointment and relief I wasn't one of them. When this op had been first mooted I had been warned off as a likely participant, and no sooner had I heard than I was being measured up for body armour, which I was cheerily assured I would definitely need.

The plan had been that we chosen few were to land on the roof of the embassy building in the second helicopter, the first having carried in our special forces who would secure the landing site. We were also told that the site was likely to be 'hot', ie still in the middle of an ongoing firefight, and I had all sorts of visions of being machine gunned on arrival or shot down by some overzealous Coalition soldier as we flew in. So I wasn't *too* disappointed not to be going! As it happened, the Iraqis had fled by the time our chaps got there and there was, thank goodness, no bloodshed.

By the morning of 27 February all Iraqi troops were in the process of attempting to get out of Kuwait, except for some units of their RGFC. All the routes out of Kuwait, however, were cut by the Coalition air assets, and the end result was a huge pile up of vehicles. The Iraqis were jammed on four lane highways with nowhere to go and the skies were full of every aircraft the Coalition could get into the air to destroy them.

The end result was illustrated dramatically by the television pictures of the Kuwait to Basra highway – the Highway of Death which I flew over at low level a few days later – displayed on screens all round the world. We heard through our liaison officers that some of the US pilots were sickened by the one-sided destruction that was now going on, and not for the first time the morality of such an unequal contest was called into question.

At the morning briefing General Sir Peter said he thought it would all be over in 24 – 96 hours, which filled us all with relief. The HQ 'stepped up' to Kuwait as planned as Op Trebor swung into operation, but it was carried out so secretly that nobody knew what was going on and it became a bit of a farce. In the end everybody was let in on the secret and things progressed smoothly thereafter.

For me at least, the first Gulf War stopped at 8.00 am local time on 28 February 1991. The Iraqis had now collapsed completely and were streaming back north to Baghdad, and it had got to the point where continuing to attack them, in my estimation, was no longer morally justifiable. This opinion was shared to a greater or lesser degree by most of my colleagues. Enough was enough.

We only now began to get a true feel for the scale of the Iraqi defeat, and it was enormous. We were told that they had lost 3,008 tanks, 1,856 armoured personnel carriers, and 2,140 artillery pieces, mainly abandoned in their retreat. The Americans were planning to blow up most of the abandoned Iraqi equipment, except the stuff that was to be kept for exploitation or for display purposes, the latter a euphemism for war booty. PJHQ sent out a demand for captured enemy equipment which made us all hoot with laughter, including as it did 100 T72 tanks, 100 BMP infantry fighting vehicles, and so on, which was just total cuckoo land. I think in the end we ended up with only three T72s, and even then they were stolen from the Americans if I remember correctly.

The battlefields were awash with weaponry, and every unit seemed determined to get at least one tank, plus a slack handful of other assorted lorries, small arms, and other trophies, back home to Germany or the UK to display on the regimental square or in their regimental museums. Fairly strict guidelines about all of this were issued almost immediately, but it wasn't too long after the end of hostilities that some idiot Army Air Corps (AAC) officer flew back from the Gulf into RAF Brize

Norton and presented HM Customs & Excise with two AK47 assault rifles which he wanted to import.

That piece of crass stupidity effectively queered the pitch for everyone else. I was quite keen that 4 RTR should have something or other to commemorate all the officers and men who served with other units in the Gulf, and I went to some lengths to secure a couple of ex-Iraqi rifles when I got back to Germany. I even got as far as getting display cabinets made for them, but then I lost track of them when I was next posted. To this day I don't know what became of them.

All efforts were very quickly directed (by us) towards getting out of the region as soon as was humanly possible. We had all had more than enough of the Middle East in general and Saudi Arabia in particular, and we were desperate to get home. Optimism soared as we began to calculate just how soon we might be able to leave Saudi Arabia. Some said as soon as within six weeks, assuming the first of 7 Armd Bde could move in about ten days time, working on the ancient army principle of first in, first out. There was a definite sense of *fin-de-siecle*, and it seemed all we had to do was exchange prisoners-of-war quickly, extract all our stuff, and we were *offski*. Brilliant. We couldn't wait.

There was another side, a darker and less happy one. The division reported that it was finding living on the battlefield a very harrowing experience. They found themselves amongst long columns of burnt out enemy vehicles, full of Iraqi dead, and the enemy prisoners they had taken were stuck out in the middle of the desert with little shelter. The realisation had also begun to dawn that the ratio of reported casualties did not really paint the picture of a hard fought campaign. The Coalition had suffered 'only' 200 or so dead, whereas figures of up to 100,000 were being quoted for the Iraqis.

I had an interesting conversation with one of our press briefers, a man for whom hitherto I had had little time, on the morality of continuing to attack a defeated enemy. I always remembered a veteran CO of the Falklands War, David Chaundler, who had subsequently taught me at staff college, describing how he had ordered his men to stop firing on retreating Argentinians after one of the battles around Port Stanley because, as he had put it, it was no longer morally sustainable.

I had been mightily impressed by this. Ten years later the same dilemma was taxing a number of people, and this briefer was of the opinion that the last twenty-four hours of our current war had been quite unnecessary. I agreed. It was rather like one of the old colonial wars I thought, where spear and shield waving charging natives had been mown down by modern rifle fire. As Hillaire Belloc famously wrote:

'Whatever happens, we have got
The Maxim gun, and they have not.'

The conflict had turned out to be a bit too one-sided for my peace of mind.

Within twenty-four hours of the cessation of hostilities I had one of my all too rare days off. When we had first arrived in Riyadh there had been far too much to do to afford such a luxury, and we had worked all day every day. Within a month or so, however, it had become clear that we were going to become stale and fed up very quickly if we continued in this vein, so every so often we got a break.

The problem was, though, that there wasn't that much for us to do outside working. Generally speaking nobody else was off at the same time, so there was little opportunity to go off in company to play sport, explore, go shopping, or whatever. Riyadh wasn't exactly conducive to R&R, being a bit of an urban wasteland of motorways on concrete stilts and unfriendly high rise office blocks in the American idiom. Reminiscent of central Birmingham, perhaps, minus women and bars and with the heating turned fully on.

I tended, therefore, to stay in the Marriott, catching up on my sleep, writing interminable letters home, and reading the many books sent to me by friends, family, and well wishers. There was an outdoor swimming pool and the weather was usually good enough to sit outside and do a little sunbathing. The pool was always swarming with RAF personnel, who I have to say provided some of the most egregious examples of scruffy servicemen in uniform that I have ever seen, anywhere. I was constantly amazed that their officers never did anything about it. Perhaps they didn't care.

The hotel itself was depressing. It wasn't that it was uncomfortable, because it was as good as any hotel of that type I've stayed in, but it had no soul. There was nowhere to go outside your room, and on venturing out regardless there was only ever a gaggle of Saudi and Kuwaiti men drinking endless cups of coffee in all male family groups. The corridors and foyers were full of noisy, chattering Kuwaiti refugee children at all hours of the day and night; mind you, they didn't have anywhere to go either until they could go back home so it was hardly their fault.

Worst of all was the television. I still have bad dreams about Saudi television, with its (to our eyes) hopelessly amateur Saudi programmes and a staple diet of overwhelmingly mediocre, and heavily censored, programmes imported from the USA. These were interrupted several times a day by the call to prayer, and nothing wrong with that, except if you were watching a film it would keep running during prayer time behind the schedule and therefore you always rejoined it having lost about five minutes of the plot! Saudi TV would undoubtedly have driven me to drink had any been available.

After my day off I returned to work with the day shift, a welcome relief after seven weeks of constant nightshift. There was now very little for me to do. 'All out in forty-two days!' became the cry, but for the moment we all sat around waiting for something to happen. I moved back to my equipment-orientated job as a host of related matters now came to hand. Not least of these was the urgent need to find out how our and the Iraqis' equipment had actually worked in reality.

A number of data collection organisations then moved into theatre to glean the relevant information. Rather uncharitably, perhaps, we saw them as overly keen to get in on the act and play desert warriors before it was all over. This was one of the great paradoxes of the time; the Gulf was full of people like me whose only thought was to get out as quickly as was humanly possible, whilst elsewhere there were scores of people who were quite desperate to get involved. I remember a Johnny-come-lately in my own regiment telling me how lucky he thought I was to have been there all through the war, and me thinking how daft he was. I would have swapped with him any time to be honest.

Chapter 20

With the war over, life became increasingly tedious as we all waited to hear when we might be able to go home. However, one important task we had to complete was the compilation of the post operations report (POR). Like many other organisations, the British army tries hard to review what has happened in training or on operations to collect the lessons learned for future endeavours. Unlike the fire services or the police, say, the army may only ply its true trade intermittently, and when it does it's always useful to know what went right, or indeed wrong.

The problem is, of course, that there is no guarantee that the next war will be the same as the one before, and it's probably fair to say that the army often enters the next war perfectly prepared for the last one. The Second World War is probably the most egregious example of this, but much the same could be said of subsequent adventures in Iraq and Afghanistan. There is no easy solution to the conundrum. Nevertheless, it would be a foolish organisation which did not at least attempt to learn lessons from past successes and failures, so we set to. A team of about twenty or so assorted arms and services representatives was sent forward from HQBFME in Riyadh to visit the British units in the field and quiz those who had been closest involved in the fighting before memories dulled.

So we flew from Riyadh to Al Jubail in an RAF Hercules, which was pleasant enough, but it was raining when we arrived at our interim stop. The aircraft then developed a fault and we could well have become stuck. If it had been peacetime we undoubtedly would have been, for the RAF was notoriously slow and inefficient in those days when it came to fixing their passenger transport aircraft. However, one of the joys of being on operations was that air transport was able to throw off the shackles of peacetime procedures and operate properly. If you wanted to go somewhere, and there was a plane going there with some room on it, you got on, as simple as that. The loadmaster might ask you if your gun was unloaded before you boarded, but that was it. What a relief it was from the tiresome bureaucracy of RAF peacetime transport arrangements!

Anyway, there was a Royal New Zealand Air Force (RNZAF) Hercules on the strip and it was available for tasking, so we transferred to that lock, stock, and barrel for onward passage to Kuwait International after a two hour pause. The NZ crew were a bit hacked off, to be honest, because they had been about to go off duty after a normal shift, but they hid it very well. They had an extremely laconic Sergeant Loadmaster who addressed everyone as 'mate', of course, who rather amusingly apologised for the lack of an in-flight movie during his pre-flight briefing, a joke I suspect he had told numerous times before, but it made me laugh anyway.

In the end they delivered us safely and without further incident to Kuwait International, despite the restricted visibility from the oil wells the Iraqis had set alight during their retreat, and we were all very grateful. The airport was a mess and presented a desolate spectacle as we deplaned. There was a burned out airliner close to our arrival point and the runways were strewn with shrapnel. Every pane of glass in the large terminal building seemed to have been broken and it looked as if the place had been thoroughly looted. We didn't have time to explore further, though, for shortly we heard the clatter of helicopters, and two or three RAF Puma aircraft hove into view, landed, and taxied up to collect us. Our party then split into smaller groups and headed off to visit various units scattered across northern Kuwait. I and several others were bound for the 1 (UK) Armd Div HQ, located some dozen miles or so beyond the outskirts of Kuwait City, on the way north to the Iraq border and Basra.

As we flew across the city I noticed that there were quite a few abandoned Iraqi tanks and other vehicles by the sides of the roads, both in the centre of the town and in the residential suburbs. Nothing had prepared me, though, for the scene outside the city on the main highway north. We flew at about 200 feet over what had become known as Death's Acre or the Highway of Death – the few kilometres of the motorway where Coalition aircraft had trapped the fleeing Iraqis and destroyed everything in continuous air attacks.

Although I had previously seen television pictures of the carnage, the reality was much worse. All lanes of the highway were blocked by destroyed and burnt-out vehicles, noses pointing north, and the roadsides and far out into the desert were littered with the detritus of a defeated army in headlong flight. The Iraqis had clearly commandeered anything that moved in their panic to escape, for amongst the tanks and trucks were large numbers of civilian cars, vans, and buses, similarly blackened by fire. Worse still, in many ways, was the evidence that all these derelict vehicles had been thoroughly looted, for each wreck was surrounded by a little pitiful pile of possessions which lay where the scavengers had discarded them. More than anything it was reminiscent of a large refuse dump, and to view it was hardly an uplifting experience. There was certainly no sense of triumph or victory as we flew over.

Our Div HQ was in a plantation on the coast just north of Kuwait City, comfortable enough as far as living in the desert goes. It consisted of the usual ops tent complex, plus a ragtag collection of tents, trucks, and assorted military and civilian vehicles parked in among the scruffy palm trees. I knew quite a number of the staff, and they seemed to be in fine fettle, if a little weary, and very pleased it was all over. I spent some time working with them, and then turned in for the night in a small tent shared with two others, a tight squeeze exacerbated by the fact there seemed to be a complete arsenal of captured Iraqi weaponry in there too!

The next day I headed back to Kuwait airport, driven by regimental chum Duncan MacMillan, who had been seconded to Div HQ as a watchkeeper, in a civvy Range Rover that he had purloined from somewhere. I bade him farewell at the terminal and would next see him back in Germany. I found my way to what temporised as a check-in desk where a cheerful RAF corporal with his feet up on the desk invited me to dump any illicit Iraqi weaponry I had on me in a box next to him and then allocated me to an aircraft. This last action wasn't too difficult for him, for there was a strictly limited number of destinations and as I said previously if there was a flight going in your direction you got on it.

The same friendly NZ Hercules crew were flying me again, and my fellow passengers included a company of QOHldrs who had just come out of the desert (and were exhausted) plus a few other odd individuals. There was also an extraordinarily pretty blonde American girl on board, from one of their National Guard units I think. Halfway through the trip to Al Jubail she disappeared into the crew cabin, and after about five minutes the aircraft began a series of turning and banking manoeuvres which the routine flight didn't call for.

Sure enough, the girl was the pilot's current *par amour* and he was taking the opportunity to give her some impromptu flying lessons, allowing her to take control (under supervision I hope). I wouldn't imagine for one minute that such practices were allowed even in the RNZAF, but nobody complained – we were all too tired anyway – and no-one in authority was ever the wiser. It made for an interesting interlude on an otherwise rather dull journey, and I was sad to see her leave the plane at Jubail.

The remainder of the flight back to Riyadh was uneventful. My old friend from staff college Jonathan Campbell-James was on the same flight and had arranged for a driver from the British Embassy to pick him up at the airport, so he kindly offered to give me a lift into town. On the way we diverted to his house inside the embassy compound for a couple of real beers before his driver deposited me back at the Marriott. This was to be my last trip up country, and the next time I saw the airport was to be on my way out of Saudi Arabia. The boys in the desert, meanwhile, had a little bit more time to kick their heels before they too headed back home.

After the trip to Kuwait, HQBFME had the distinct feel of end of term about it. However, believe it or not, we were still finalising the procurement of some of the Urgent Operational Requirements (UORs) which hadn't been delivered in time for the war. In particular, the artillery smoke rounds I had sourced from South Africa – still a pariah state as most of the international community was concerned – eventually turned up, all 5,000 of them, but they were never used. I dare say they're still in some ammo store somewhere ready to be used, or maybe they were fired during the more recent military adventures in Afghanistan and/or Iraq (again).

It had become clear that it wasn't just the purchase of the smoke rounds which had been unnecessary. Vast amounts of kit had been sent out to Saudi Arabia but never used, either because nobody knew where it was or because it had disappeared. The main depot in theatre, 62 Ordnance Company, had expanded to cover many acres and there were literally thousands of containers and boxes there. Many of these were never even opened, much less logged and distributed. Some front line units had become so frustrated by the usual supply system, which had been overwhelmed by the scale of the task, that they had resorted to sending their own men back to the depot to find the bits and pieces they so desperately needed. This further exacerbated the problems, because now there were additional bodies rooting through the opened boxes looking for what they wanted.

If any lesson was going to be taken from the Gulf War it had to be the pressing requirement for a comprehensive stock monitoring and tracking system to enable the army to keep tabs on what had been sent and where it was stored. No doubt there's some sort of barcode scheme nowadays, but it got to the point where we were never actually completely sure, for example, of how many tanks we had in theatre.

We did have a little bit of fun on the social side, however, as the permanent expatriate Brits in Riyadh kindly did their level best to entertain as many of us as possible. For our part, we were free to move around Riyadh again and had the free time to do it. On one memorable occasion, a few of us were invited down to the Diplomatic Quarter to the residence of one of the British military representatives for a cocktail party. Also at this party was a smattering of nurses from 205 Field Hospital, a TA unit which recruited in the Glasgow area.

This organisation had been mobilised and sent out to the Gulf in January, and at least one of the flights carrying its personnel had arrived at King Khaled International airport in Riyadh in the middle of a SCUD raid. This was indeed an unfortunate baptism of fire; it's bad enough arriving in a strange country in the middle of the night, but to do so in the middle of a missile raid and have to scramble into your NBC kit the minute you hit the tarmac is doubly unfortunate.

It didn't seem to have caused the nurses at the party any permanent harm, though, and they were in fine spirits. We spent a very pleasant evening in their company, were careful with our alcohol intake, thanked our host and left. Our erstwhile companions, on the other hand, were not so abstemious and took full advantage of the drink supplied, having been teetotal since their arrival in the country. An unfortunate and embarrassing episode then ensued as they too took their leave; whilst shaking hands with her hostess on saying goodbye, one of the nurses let two cans of beer tumble from where she had concealed them under her coat. We were mortified at this violation of our hosts' hospitality, but they never batted an eyelid.

Time came to thin out personnel in the HQ. Extraordinarily, we were informed that individuals would not be told directly that they were surplus to requirements, but that if their names did not appear on the next day's duty roster they could assume that was the case. What a ham-handed way to deal with drawdown, I thought, and it was very poor man management. I have to admit, though, that despite the manner in which the information was disseminated, I was more than delighted when my name did not appear on the duty list. I could go!

On 10 March I got final confirmation that my services were indeed no longer required and I started to make preparations to leave. The procedure was actually quite easy; the transport and movement gurus were in the same building and I simply had to find the first flight with space on it and book myself on as a passenger. That done, all I had to do was wait, in my case for only four days. I handed in my trusty NBC kit and posted my temperate green and brown combat kit back to Germany, thereby ensuring that I'd have no option but to swank back in my desert kit. I reckoned that was the very least I was entitled to after a three month enforced sojourn in the Middle East.

Notwithstanding that my name was firmly on the flight manifest, bitter experience of past RAF transport movements had taught generations of servicemen not to expect anything to happen until it actually happens. That final night in the Marriott one of my compatriots opened a specially hoarded bottle of contraband whisky in celebration, which was very generous as he himself had a few weeks to go before he was repatriated.

Finally, after what seemed like an age of waiting, my last day in Saudi Arabia arrived. I have to be honest and say I felt not one iota of sadness or nostalgia at the thought of leaving. I said my goodbyes in HQBFME without too much fuss. Farewells in the services are never very emotional events because they are a normal part of everyday life and therefore expected. With a posting system that moved people around roughly every two years you can't afford the luxury of heart-wrenching farewells. In any case, I would meet up with these people again, so I just shook hands with everyone and left.

Typically, the flight left at 2.20 am local time – the middle of the night again. Thus my little adventure ended as it had begun, at possibly the most unedifying time for any journey. I was also pretty sceptical that the flight would leave on time, for the one the night before had been five hours late. But to my pleasant surprise there was no real problem. Takeoff was only forty minutes late, and the plane was a civvy one – British Airways doing their bit to take the boys and girls home.

The atmosphere on the flight was understandably jolly as all passengers were just delighted at getting out. For the first time in my experience on a military flight we were handed a tin of beer and half a bottle of wine each, which of course added to the festive air. Obviously some wise individual had worked out that the dangers of drunken mayhem on board flights out of Saudi were infinitesimally small compared to the dangers of soldiers denied any alcohol over many months hitting the town centres of Europe and over-indulging.

Accordingly, it appeared that a pre-emptive strike had been authorised, so to speak. It was probably a very sensible move, for it took the edge off many ambitions to drink the nearest bar dry on return to civilisation. The immediate practical result, however, was to send everybody on the flight to sleep within about forty-five minutes of takeoff, and most remained that way until touchdown in Germany at RAF Wildenrath some hours later.

I was delighted to find the CO's staff car, plus driver, waiting for me. I loaded all my gear into the boot of the car as quickly as I could and we were off, me rather self-consciously wearing my 9 mm pistol plus ammunition on my belt. It was a long two and a half hour drive and I felt a bit odd in my sand coloured desert combat uniform as we sped past the damp green fields of the German farmland. But soon enough I was standing on my own front doorstep and just pleased to be home at last.

In retrospect, had it all been worth it? On balance I thought not, and I still harboured doubts over the morality of the whole escapade. I guess I'd have been more content if I had seen anything that had warmed me to the people and societies of that particular region, but I had not. But we had done what we had been asked to do, for better or for worse, and that would have to be sufficient for the time being.

Chapter 21

Although none of us thought overmuch about the last few months in the Middle East, I was left with three very strong and abiding impressions from my time there. The first was that the Iraqis had been much poorer soldiers, and therefore a much less dangerous enemy, than we had been led to believe. It is, of course, one of the cardinal sins of soldiering to underestimate your enemy, but I would contend that it is almost as bad to overestimate him. While I am prepared to accept that until we knew better we were quite right to regard the Iraqi forces as equivalent to our own, we should surely have been more honest with ourselves and the rest of the world as the conflict unfolded.

The Coalition *must* have realised fairly early on that it was not up against a peer enemy. I refuse to believe that those directing the war did not know this, and still wonder what political imperative kept this from the rest of us. Perhaps the information was withheld to maintain the integrity of the Coalition itself, or more probably to keep public support, and particularly that of the American public, without whose backing the alliance would surely have collapsed. Whatever the reason, the truth was that the Iraqi troops were never anything more than a third world army, dressed up in first world equipment perhaps, who had about as much chance of defeating the Coalition as the Dervishes had of trouncing the British at Omdurman.

Secondly, and with apologies to my colleagues and comrades who had served in the front line, I (and many others) thought our division had been slow and ponderous in its operations and had never quite risen to the occasion. Too many years training to defeat the Warsaw Pact in northern Germany in a series of set piece battles seemed to have drained it of dash and initiative. True, there had been a series of frustrating delays at the border whilst the Americans breached the minefields and berm to let our division through, which made for a slow start. But that obstacle having been overcome, it should have allowed us to take full part in the breakneck dash into Iraq.

Instead, while the Americans threw caution to the wind when they began to realise the full extent of the victory, we were plodding our steady way through a series of half-heartedly held Iraqi defensive positions and complaining of being held up by hordes of prisoners when the enemy started surrendering in droves. I don't think there was much wrong with our soldiers, who did everything that was asked of them and more, nor was our equipment responsible for our fairly lacklustre performance. But I did wonder whether we really had a feel for how to breed the sort of commanders we needed for this sort of high speed, intuitive, seat-of-the-pants type of warfare. Fear of making a mistake has been a flaw in many of our senior commanders through history, and perhaps the over-riding desire to have everything 'properly teed up', to use Montgomery's phrase, prevented the division and its two brigades being bold and decisive in its actions.

Finally, I had been most impressed by the competence of our American allies, who were the cornerstone of the Coalition and whose victory it really was. They had proved to be both thoroughly meticulous and professional in their planning, and then had prosecuted their plan with boldness and imagination. They appeared to have none of that air of enthusiastic amateurism which we Brits still admire in our military, and they were considerably the better for it. When presented with tactical and operational opportunities demanding instant decision and action, they had the self confidence and breadth of vision to seize the moment.

Whether they had to prosecute the war quite so determinedly right to the bitter end is open to debate, but there could be no doubting their determination and tenacity. Man for man (or woman for woman) I have always been of the opinion that the British soldier is a little bit superior to his American counterpart, and up to brigade level we could probably give them a run for their money, but at division and above I don't think we can compete. In the Gulf they were motivated, superbly equipped, and well led, and as long as they enjoyed the support of the American public they probably had no equal. They won the war with everybody else just really tagging along, and in doing so laid the ghost of Vietnam.

I went on leave almost immediately, as we had all been promised whilst out in the Gulf. Just before departing there was a curry lunch held in the officers' mess for the Gulf veterans, all of whom had come home safely, thank goodness, in the space of a few days. I think that was the point where the war quite clearly came to an end for me, for it was all so normal it appeared that nothing had happened in the interim period at all.

My holiday was a combination of gentle tourism and visiting people I hadn't seen for a while. I quickly christened it, tongue-in-cheek, as the 'victory tour', for that's what it felt like some of the time for sure. Most people had seen the vivid TV images of the bombing attacks on Baghdad, which had been pretty serious looking stuff, so I have difficulty persuading them that, for me in Riyadh at least, it hadn't been very dangerous at all. And every conversation seemed to be prefaced by 'I know you won't want to talk about it', but I was very happy to do so, for it had been an unusual experience.

In all I had about five weeks' leave to savour, and then returned to barracks in Germany. It was, in fact, quite strange to be back to normal peacetime soldiering and all its niceties. For the first time, perhaps, I was aware of the trivial nature of much of the stuff we did, and sometimes struggled to get excited about matters which obviously agitated others but to me seemed relatively unimportant. My days were quickly filled by a plethora of matters ranging from training, discipline, and financial matters, all the way down to the mundane reports and returns which are the bête noire of all desk-bound regimental officers.

For 4 RTR in Germany life slowly returned to normal, and the long, slow haul to get our fifty-seven tanks operational again began. Eventually it was completed, but it took another year or so, and other forces beyond our control had been at work in the meantime. The Government published its Options for Change strategy for the armed forces, which was a defence review by any other name, and 4 RTR did not appear on the new order of battle. We knew we were to be amalgamated or disbanded, and things were never the same again. In the end, the regiment slaved over its obsolescent Chieftains to get them fit for Hohne Ranges one more time, fired them during the last gunnery camp, and then handed them over to be scrapped. It was very sad, and an enormous effort for nothing.

And it wasn't just the equipment which was scrapped; large scale troop reductions were also required (sound familiar?) and the army set forth on a round of voluntary and compulsory redundancies. Within twelve months of our return from the Gulf, two thirds of the dozen or so regimental officers who had gone to war had left the army. Most of them were forced to go, victims of their SSCs, which in normal times might have been converted to regular commissions for those who wanted to stay longer term.

Funnily enough, those who had seen action were mainly SSC officers, and therefore those forced to retire were the very ones who had all the combat experience. Arguably we ended up with a remaining officers corps experienced in orderly officer duties, barrack administration, and not a lot else. It was a crass decision, and I can think of no competent large scale commercial organisation which would approach a similar problem by sacking its most successful and experienced salesmen, for example. At a stroke the RTR lost most of the operational experience in tank warfare amongst its officers.

In what I thought was a fitting, and slightly tongue in cheek, finale to the whole Gulf saga, the Gulf officer veterans presented one of the signed prints of the Terence Cuneo oil painting, which had been commissioned by 1 UK Armd Div, to the 4 RTR officers' mess. Rather cheekily, we had a plaque placed on it with the legend 'Presented By The Officers Who Went To The Gulf To Those Who Did Not', which raised a wry smile and was generally taken in the good humour intended. Then, after a few weeks, most of the decent war stories had been told, and talk of the war quietly died away.

Chapter 22

A few weeks later there I was, sitting at my desk in RHQ 4 RTR in Imphal Barracks, Osnabruck, Germany, doing some bit of administration or other, when my phone rang. On the other end was Eyre Maunsell, a 4 RTR officer seconded to the army's personnel branch in the UK, and he had a very simple question for me; would I like to attend the US Army's staff college in the USA? It took me all of three seconds to say yes.

Now, having already graduated from the British staff college at Camberley some years previously it was unusual, but not unique, to be offered the chance of attending an overseas staff college as well. But joining the small band of 'Double Blues', as it were, was an attractive proposition. The regimental hierarchy thought otherwise, for it interfered with their planning, and after I heard nothing for a couple of weeks I phoned Eyre back and asked him what the score was. I was somewhat taken aback to learn that he had been told that I had changed my mind and no longer wanted to go.

This was not the first time that my aspirations within the army had been thwarted by sleight of hand and I wasn't going to let it happen again. So, after a bit of to-ing and fro-ing I got my wish and my posting to the USA was confirmed. It was, on mature reflection, a bit of a jolly as I had no need of the additional qualification for career purposes, nor was I persuaded that I had been specially selected in any way. It was simply that there was a posting to be filled and I fitted the bill. But no complaints from me!

As you can imagine there was quite a bit of admin involved, not least of which was packing up the house and sending off all our belongings by ship to the USA. Thankfully there was a well practised system in place for doing so and it was pretty seamless, but it meant roughly six weeks without possessions. I then went on leave, back to Scotland to see my folks and family.

There was one slight problem. I had recently bought a brand new BMW 325i Cabriolet under the tax free arrangements in place at the time, and now I was posted out of Germany I hadn't kept the car out of the UK for long enough to satisfy the tax free regulations. I had planned to leave the car with my Dad for him to drive for the year I would be away. So he and I toddled down to our local HMRC office and were completely honest about our dilemma, with the potential tax bill coming to several thousand pounds. I was very pleased that we were able to come to a mutually agreeable arrangement and I got off fairly lightly!

I flew from RAF Brize Norton in Oxfordshire, if I remember correctly, to Washington DC in an RAF VC-10. For once the RAF was on the ball and there were no delays or hitches, probably because the pilots had remembered to set their alarm clocks at their nearby luxury hotel this time. I have mentioned before that all the seats in the aircraft faced towards the back, I presume for safety reasons, from where came the description 'Backwards Airways'. The same epithet could easily be applied for other reasons too, of course. As it was, the flight was uneventful and we were met at the scrum in arrivals at Dulles airport by an official from the British Embassy and escorted to the hotel in Crystal City where I was to stay for a couple of days for briefings before onward transit.

I can't actually remember what the briefings were all about except I wasn't to lose sight of the fact I was representing the UK whilst in the US. Allowances that I was entitled to certainly formed part of the package, of which more later. I did have some spare time to look around Washington though, which I had visited previously. I always liked the atmosphere of the city, especially Georgetown, and it struck me in ambience, if not in architecture, as a rather warmer Edinburgh. After a few days it was back to the airport and on my way.

The United States Army Command & General Staff College (USACGSC) which I was to attend is located in Fort Leavenworth, Kansas. The state of Kansas, as many will be aware, is about the size of France but at that time only had a population of *circa* two and a half million, so sparsely populated doesn't really cover it. The flight time there from Washington non-stop is about two and three quarter hours which gives you some idea of the scale of the USA – it did for me anyway. On arrival I was met by my sponsors for the duration of my stay.

A word on sponsors. Each overseas student was allocated three sets of sponsor families; two civilian and one military. Their purpose was to welcome those who came to Fort Leavenworth from outwith the US, make us feel welcome, introduce us to their local communities, and generally help us to settle down.

My civilian sponsors were utterly charming and kind and I still remember them fondly.

My military sponsors I already knew well, because by one of those strange quirks of fate they turned out to be none other than Colonel Tom Brown, US Army, and his lovely wife Barbara. Now Tom had commanded C Squadron 4 RTR in Tidworth in 1983-84, on attachment from the US army, and I was one of the welcoming party when he arrived in the UK for that posting. In classic 4 RTR officers' mess fashion I had driven up to Heathrow to meet him and his family on arrival, and of course his flight landed at Gatwick. But that minor difficulty was soon overcome and he and Barbara spent, I hope, a very happy couple of years with us.

Now the roles were reversed, and I'm happy to report that Tom managed to get to the right airport! As the British representative I was provided with an allowance to stay for a fortnight in a local hotel whilst I arranged to rent a house, buy a car, and so on. But Tom and Barbara wouldn't hear of it and insisted that I stay with them instead, which of course was infinitely more enjoyable. However, it did leave me in the position where I had been given a considerable sum of money by the British Embassy to pay for something I did not require.

This smacked of fraud to me, so I phoned the embassy and told them I would have to hand the money back to them. The senior warrant officer I spoke to in the pay team was taken aback; nobody, he told me, had *ever* tried to pay back any allowances they had been given. Indeed, he went on, there was no mechanism for doing so. There then ensued an increasingly surreal conversation in which he tried to justify why it would be all right for me to keep the money. Eventually he asked whether I had taken my hosts out for a meal, or had even bought them a bottle of wine as a present. When I replied that I had, he then triumphantly concluded that clearly this relatively modest expenditure justified the considerably larger amount of allowance, and that everything was accordingly in order. So that was all OK then!

Shortly thereafter I found a house to rent and moved in to await the arrival of our possessions from Germany. I also bought my predecessor-in-post's car, which was almost inevitably a mistake as it broke down expensively shortly after his departure. Some things you never learn. I had a couple of weeks' leave before the start of the course and drove west across Kansas, a seemingly endless journey across the prairie where, I can assure you, the corn is indeed as high as an elephant's eye, just like they say.

My new car gave up the ghost just short of the Colorado border, and I would have been stranded there had it not been for the kindness of a total stranger who lent me his second car so I could continue my journey whilst my car was being fixed. Once again I was struck by the incredible generosity shown to me by the American people, and only hoped that we were as kind to them when they came to the UK. Colorado is very picturesque and lovely, and I was only unnerved by the almost total lack of traffic on the roads through the mountains. It did at times feel like the edge of the world.

Refreshed after my all too brief holiday, I returned to Leavenworth and got myself sorted out for the start of the course. Fort Leavenworth was founded in 1827 and is situated on a strategic bend in the Missouri River, on whose banks you can still discern the ruts made by the wagons of the earliest settlers if you know where to look, and it's where as previously stated the USACGSC is located. The contiguous county town of Leavenworth, to which the fort has given its name, is a typical small mid-western town of roughly 36,000 souls. Leavenworth's main claim to fame is the number of prisons it boasts, including the federal US Penitentiary, Leavenworth, and the US Disciplinary Barracks, the US Army's only maximum security prison. Although these institutions give the town a somewhat severe façade, it is a pleasant place to live and work, and not too far from Kansas City for those who seek a bigger environment and brighter lights.

Rather naively I had assumed that being a fort it would have a guarded perimeter, or perhaps even a traditional, historic palisade curtilage like those featured in every western film you have ever seen, but not so. It is more of a cantonment than a fort, at least it was in those pre-9/11 days, and open on all sides. It is also home to several other US Army schools and colleges and has the reputation of being 'the intellectual center (sic) of the US Army'.

Where do I begin to describe the US Army staff course? Well, for starters, there were 1,280 students on the course I attended, about ten times the number of the equivalent British course then at Camberley. The vast majority were, unsurprisingly, Americans drawn from all four of their services – US Navy, Army, Airforce and Marines. We 'international students', as we were called, numbered about seventy if

I remember correctly and I was the sole UK representative. The course also included the first Russian and first Ukrainian army officers, part of the general rapprochement following the dissolution of the Warsaw Pact.

The course itself followed the usual curriculum on doctrine, tactics, and leadership and was taught mainly in small syndicate groups of about ten, presided over by a US Army lieutenant colonel (British abbreviation Lt Col, American LTC; don't get me started on Americanisms …). I have to say I was very impressed by my new American colleagues on the whole. They were very professional if a tad serious but were good at what they did. There was an enormous amount of reading doled out as part of the course, and I warmed to them even more when one of them whispered in class to me 'it's only a lot of reading if you actually do it'. My sort of people!

There were, of course, many aspects that I found quite amusing, in a laugh-with-them rather than a laugh-at-them kind of way. One that struck me straight away was that it was impossible for me at first to distinguish very senior American officers from their lowlier compatriots. They all wore the same uniform, and sometimes the only indicator of rank would be a discreet five stars (that's pretty senior by the way) hidden on a rank slide on a uniform indistinguishable from everybody else's. Addressing the US Army's Chief of Staff as 'mate' as you politely ask him to get out of the way is not seen as best practice, not in anyone's army, but you couldn't tell.

They also had a pathological fascination with getting their hair cut. The onsite barbers seemed to be at it day and night, with queues of US army officers outside its door waiting for their already extraordinarily short hair to be shorn even shorter. It was a bit like a skinheads' convention at times, without the big boots and tattoos. Meanwhile we Europeans were swanning around the campus in our strange and outlandish uniforms tucking our flowing locks into our berets. To be honest, much of the time I made my uniform up; whatever was comfortable or clean would do in any combination. Who knew otherwise?

The hours that many of them kept were also a source of constant amazement. It was not unusual for the US students on the course to be in work at 5.00 am, which was close to when some of the international officers were just going to bed. In the evening they would turn in at 9.30 pm, which was before many of us had had our evening meal, ready to get up fresh and eager for the next working day. We just couldn't understand it, but each to their own I guess.

However I must say again just how welcoming, pleasant, and kind our hosts were. And they too must have been amused by us much of the time. When at work my American chums seemed to be unfazed by anything they were asked to do or any role they were asked to play. Tell a British student at one of the UK staff colleges at a map exercise that they're to fill the role of corps commander and they'll have kittens; tell an American the same thing and they'll deal with it exactly the same as they would if asked to command a platoon. They were, and probably still are, much more comfortable at scale than we are.

We had a couple of trips within the USA as part of the course and they were good fun; not quite as hedonistic as similar trips undertaken by the British staff college back in the day but fun nonetheless. The detail is lost to me now, but I do remember one aspect of a trip to Washington DC, where we visited the Pentagon and similar institutions. One of our number, a Kiwi SAS officer and serious rugby player, took great delight in saying to everyone we met in the streets wearing a back-to-front baseball cap – which was virtually every male under twenty-five – 'excuse me, do you realise you're wearing your hat the wrong way round?', which provided endless, childish amusement. Looking at him it was clear that no-one was going to take umbrage.

There was much greater emphasis on the reading of military history than there had been at Camberley as far as I can remember. Our first piece of required reading was *The Killer Angels*, a historical novel by Michael Shaara that was awarded the Pulitzer Prize for Fiction in 1975. The book depicts the three days of the Battle of Gettysburg during the American Civil War, much of it told through the real life character Colonel Joshua Lawrence Chamberlain of Maine, whose 20th Maine Volunteer Infantry Regiment held the left of the Union line during the battle and whose defence of a feature known as Little Round Top was critical to the defeat of the Confederate Army.

We visited the battlefield, and stood on Little Round Top, which was a sobering but fascinating experience. I was also able during my time in Leavenworth to research and present to my classmates on the Battle of Caporetto (aka Twelfth Battle of the Isonzo) in 1917, a heavy Italian defeat at the hands of the Germans and Austrians, of particular interest to me because, as previously mentioned, my grandfather had been there. Few people realise that there were British troops fighting in Italy in the First World War, but there were. My grandfather was part of an all volunteer medical unit which he had joined with all his pals, as they did in those days. Typically, he never spoke very much about it, except to say that he had been 'the first man in the retreat' and his Italian comrades had all thrown their rifles in the canal and run away. Perhaps they had learned that a German officer called Rommel was one of those attacking them!

The senior American officers who came to speak to us were very impressive. Many of them had served in the Vietnam War and were grizzled old veterans, and some had also been involved in Desert Storm in 1991. They tended to bounce on to the stage in the vast central auditorium deep in the college and shout out the name of the syndicate they had been part of when they had attended in the past. This usually resulted in the current iteration of that syndicate jumping to their feet and shouting 'Hooaah!' in the way that American soldiers tend to do. It was great theatre, and the generals were great speakers, much better than their British equivalents in my opinion.

The course was overall a very busy and comprehensive one and thoroughly enjoyable for me and my fellow international officers. It wasn't all work, of course, and away from the course there were a myriad of other social, sporting, and cultural events which went on. Some of them were great fun to take part in and showed colourful aspects of mid-western life which were, in some cases, not too far from the Hollywood images so familiar to all of us.

Chapter 23

Away from the course at Leavenworth there was an awful lot of extra-curricular activity going on, much of it thanks to our civilian sponsors who took their volunteer jobs seriously and made sure we were well entertained.

Kansas had, to my European perceptions at least, pretty extreme weather. The summer was hot, sometimes very hot, and the winters freezing and with snow often up to two feet thick or more. Every now and then there would be a tremendous storm with deafening thunder and dramatic lightning accompanied by torrential rain. More eerily, in tornado season the sky might turn green, indicating the distinct possibility that one of these damaging events might happen. Thankfully it never did when I was there.

In the summer months I lost count of the number of barbeques and 'cook outs' I was invited to by my hosts. Because the summer weather tended to be pretty predictable and pleasant, they could be planned weeks ahead and were great fun. Sometimes they were in a neighbour's back garden – sorry, back yard of course – or part and parcel of a bigger event, like sports or other public occasions.

Talking of sports, I got full exposure to the complete gamut of American sporting activities. American football remains a mystery to me, but I enjoyed hugely the razzamatazz that accompanies it, even at local level. In these modern politically correct times I shall forego any comment on the cheerleaders except to say they were lovely to behold. Some are critical of the stop-go rhythm of the game, but I found it most interesting. What I did enjoy immensely was the whole feeling of occasion, and that it was truly a family activity, which sadly we cannot claim for our own football (soccer) which is still blighted by bad behaviour and hooliganism all too often.

I had a better understanding of baseball having played rounders before at school. Whilst I was never completely *au fait* with the intricacies of the game I understood most of the basics. It was great fun to go with Tom and Barbara Brown, my great friends and military sponsors, to watch their boys play and get a feel for what I had seen on TV and at the cinema so many times before. I got the chance to understand the context as part of the American experience, which was most educational.

We internationals also played friendly but always competitive games against our US colleagues. These too tended to be family occasions with barbeques and picnics and always great fun. If I remember correctly we lost heavily at American football, scored a more-or-less draw at rugby (I can't remember the exact score), and won comfortably at football. The footie rules allowed for a generous number of substitutes, and the Americans tried a sneaky tactic and subbed their entire team with ten minutes to go, knowing that we were too few in numbers of competent players to do the same. But we had a couple of South American wizards in our side who were by far and away the best players on the pitch. Plus we had a German goalkeeper. You don't lose if you have a German goalkeeper. It's just one of the basic rules of the game.

I also went to a couple of rodeos with my friends, and they were just great. Everyone in Kansas seemed to have a stetson and pair of cowboy boots in their wardrobe for such occasions, and they were present in abundance. Some of the stuff – the bull riding for example – looked outrageously dangerous to me, and I was surprised at how few injuries the participants seemed to suffer. Presumably there's a knack to it. These rodeos were an absolute carnival of colours, sounds, and smells, and if you ever get the chance to go to one grab it. Just remember to shout 'yeehah!' occasionally and you'll fit right in.

Part of our remit as international students was to 'fly the flag', so everyone took it in turns to host a party at home for as many guests as they could accommodate. Such parties had a national theme, with much bigging up of one's home country with flags and other symbols of nationhood, especially in terms of food and drink. Particularly memorable was the Italian officer's supper party where all the pasta dishes were in the green, white, and red of the Italian tricolour.

Much as I might have wished it, I'm afraid I was unable to source the ingredients for my favoured menu when it was my turn, and so my guests were spared the pie 'n'chips and deep fried Mars bar, all washed down with copious glasses of Irn Bru, that I had hoped to unleash on them, poor unsuspecting souls. In the end I had to settle for something rather more quintessentially British, and for the life of me I can't recall what that might have been. Nobody reported themselves ill afterwards, though, so it must have been OK.

Occasionally we might travel into Kansas City for other events, although in my case such forays were rare. I did venture there once, though, with my Aussie chum John Casey to see the well known Irish skiffle band and modern beat combo U2, of whom some of you may have heard. Why they named themselves after an early German submarine is anybody's guess, but that doesn't matter right now. The concert took place in a major stadium and the weather was absolutely freezing. They were awful, as in appallingly poor. Despite having front row seats we left halfway through and went home. I should have asked for my money back but forgot.

Now, in some circles bashing our transatlantic cousins has been a popular sport for as long as I can remember, whether it be for their extraordinary dress sense, extraordinary appetites, or extraordinary rendition – or perhaps all three and everything else in between. But you'll have picked up that I've always rather liked Americans in general terms, and thus follow a few words on some of the positives that have come out of the good ol' USA over the years. Let me share those I think we should be grateful to them for, in no particular order.

I had a good-natured argument with one of our colonial cousins over this the other day, but in my opinion nobody does breakfast like the Americans. Down to the diner in downtown Leavenworth at some unearthly hour in the morning, sit up at the counter, and immerse yourself in the experience. Good coffee with endless refills until you cry 'stop!', crispy bacon, 'eggs over easy', pancakes with maple syrup, *ye cannae whack it*. Kippers and kedgeree aside, it knocks spots off anything we can offer over here. Now, I haven't had breakfast in Timbuktu or Transylvania so maybe I'm just showing my lack of travel, but I'll take some convincing that anyone does breakfast better than the Yankee-Doodle-Dandies.

Next, Christmas. I don't really know if it was anything to do with the large number of Americans with German ancestry – estimated at roughly sixteen per cent of the US population or forty-nine million people – but our hosts seemed to do Christmas really well, and not in the schmaltzy way you might imagine from the movies. Just across the state border lies the small town of Weston, Missouri, pronounced 'Missoura' if you're local, a lovely historical and picturesque settlement full of antebellum houses and once the furthest west town of the US until Texas was admitted as a state in 1845. Buffalo Bill himself was once resident here, and it was a major starting point for settlers heading west to California.

I digress. All I wanted to say was that I spent some time visiting Weston during the Christmas holidays on 1992-93 and it was almost magical, so well was it decked out for the celebrations. Even the cheerful Santa Claus on the boardwalk was somehow entirely appropriate and not in the least bit slushy or over-sentimental. It was a lovely place to visit at that time of year.

And, notwithstanding our U2 concert fiasco, we do have to thank the Americans for rock 'n' roll. Funny one this one, because arguably the Americans, or white Americans at any rate, didn't really wake up to the fact they'd invented rock and roll until we Brits repackaged it in the form of the Beatles and their many imitators and exported it to back to them. But invent it they did, emerging in the southern states from a mixture of rhythm and blues, country, soul, gospel, folk and jazz music in the 1940s and 50s, espoused by musicians and singers like Chuck Berry, Elvis Presley, Buddy Holly, Jerry Lee Lewis, Little Richard, Fats Domino *et al.*

Its development went hand in hand with the adoption of the electric guitar as instrument of choice for the young. Then the Beatles got hold of it and changed it forever, in the same way as they changed more or less everything they touched in that period in the 1960s when the world changed from monochrome to colour. So hats off to our US cousins for letting us have it to play around with.

Finally, the biggest and best thing I want to thank the Americans for is my daughter, who was born there. It lets me tell everybody that 'I own an American', a gift I am eternally grateful for and will always cherish.

Chapter 24

I had always wanted to learn how to fly an aircraft. In fact, when I first went to university I applied to join the University Air Squadron (UAS). These RAF-sponsored units form a valuable part of their recruiting process and their main role is to 'attract ambitious and intelligent students into a career as an RAF officer', although joining the UAS doesn't necessarily mean you have to join the RAF afterwards.

My application went swimmingly until it came to the medical, when it was discovered (as I had rather expected if I'm honest) that the eardrum I had perforated whilst learning to swim as a lad in Govan Baths in Glasgow was still damaged. I wrote earlier how I had to get this fixed before I got into Sandhurst much later, but it effectively put the kibosh on my first attempt to become an aviator.

My second attempt was a rather half-hearted one, made a few years later when I was in my earlier days with 4th Tanks. The AAC was always on the lookout for pilot material, either on attachment from your parent unit or as a permanent transfer into the corps. Such was the requirement at the time that the official appeal for recruits stated that 'applications were not to be withheld at unit level', in other words if you wanted to go for pilot assessment your regiment couldn't stop you, in theory at least.

But dark forces within 4 RTR came into play, for my departure did not sit easily with the planned officer manning plot, and I was persuaded that I was too tall at six feet three inches to be accepted. This, I learned later, was just not true, but at the time I didn't take it any further. But when slightly older and wiser I insisted on getting my own way. The very fact that I was on the USACGSC at Fort Leavenworth at all was proof of this. I had learned how to play the game.

Imagine my great delight, then, when I discovered right at the beginning of the course that there was a flying club at the Fort based in the aptly named Sherman Airfield, which was on campus as it were. I presume the primary purpose of the airfield was always to facilitate military flights into the fort, and indeed these frequently came and went during my time there, but it was also home to civilian flying clubs too and I applied to join one with some alacrity.

The medical requirements for civilian flying were less stringent than those for the military, and everything was hunky-dory this time. I do remember having some difficulty with a couple of pages in the booklet assessing whether I had any hint of colour blindness, which runs in my family history. However the examining doctor, himself a pilot, merely said 'Of course you can see that it's an elephant amongst all those coloured bubbles', and that was that. I was good to go!

At this point I should probably mention that one of the enabling factors for me taking up my flying aspiration was the cost, which was miniscule by European standards at the time. At the time the £/$ exchange rate was two dollars to the pound, and I was still on generous overseas allowances which were calculated on the cost of living in Washington DC, not Kansas which was substantially less expensive. Against this background, the cost of an hour's instruction on one of the club's Cessna 152s, including aircraft *plus* fuel *plus* instructor came to the extraordinarily low sum of fourteen dollars!

My instructor was a civilian living in Leavenworth town, one Bob Drennan. Bob had learned to fly through the GI Bill when he had left the US forces at the end of the Second World War and was an excellent and experienced instructor. My memory may be playing tricks here, but I'm convinced that when I first met him he was wearing faded bib denim dungarees over a checked shirt like a typical farmboy. He may even have had a stalk of corn dangling from his lips, but perhaps this is just too much of a midwest cliché to possibly be true. But he was definitely a Kansas man through and through.

My first flying lesson with him scared me half to death. Safety always came first, and I had to learn what to do if the aircraft I was piloting stalled, that is got into a situation where the wings had insufficient lift and it basically stopped flying. This can happen at any time in flight dependent on conditions, but is most likely on takeoff or landing, for student pilots at least. So Bob decided to show me what stalling an aircraft felt like. He took our little Cessna 152 up to 5,000 feet and then stalled it continuously down to about 1,000 feet. It dropped like a falling leaf time and time again, and I had my heart in my mouth throughout and gripped the dashboard tightly. I truly thought I was going to die.

However, I didn't (obviously), and then it was my turn to learn how to recover the aircraft. The trick was to induce the stall by climbing higher and higher with the stall warning horn blaring until the plane stops flying and drops in the air. The drill was then to drop the nose, apply maximum safe throttle and use the rudder to correct any yaw. Or something like that, it was a long time ago. You did regain control very quickly, though, always assuming that you had enough space beneath you not to hit the ground. It became second nature after a while, which is what was intended.

Then followed, I think, an interminable series of takeoffs and landings, called 'touch and go' in the US and 'circuits and bumps' in the UK. Basically you just land and takeoff again without stopping – or stalling of course. After that, and in no particular order, we did banks and turns, level flight and trimming the aircraft, short take-offs and landings, the latter also on rough ground or unprepared airstrips, which called for the judicious use of throttle and flaps to achieve the lowest landing speeds and softest touchdowns.

This led directly on to practising emergency landings away from the airfield. The final iteration of this particular fun little number was Bob closing down the throttle whilst I was in control and looking elsewhere, and saying 'Engine's stopped. What are you going to do now?' I replied 'Well, I'd better land the damn' thing then', to which he responded 'On you go then'.

Now Kansas is mainly farmland and most of it is pretty flat, so it was fairly easy to spot a suitable field in which I could land. I went through all the drills I had been taught and was coming in for a full flaps, minimum speed landing on soft ground and was at about 100 feet off the ground when Bob said 'That's good enough, up we go again'. The training was to come in handy later though, when I did have to make an emergency landing, sort of, but you can read about that shortly.

The Holy Grail for all student pilots is to go solo, and for some it comes much sooner than for others, depending on skill and competence. For me it seemed to take longer than most, but maybe it just felt that way because I was so impatient to get up there on my own. Eventually, midway through yet another session of touch and gos, Bob asked me to stop next time and taxi to the control tower and let him out. Before leaving the aircraft he said 'Now, just you go and do three more takeoffs and landings like we've been doing', and then he was off.

Left on my own in the cockpit brought mixed emotions. The thrill of being about to go solo was electrifying but was tempered by the fear of possibly getting it all wrong. It all went fine though, tickety-boo even, and I completed the three circuits without mishap. There were congratulations all round when I got into the club house. I had soloed!

I was still, however, some way off qualifying for my Private Pilot's Licence (PPL). To do that I had to learn how to plan and file flight plans and complete three solo cross-county flights, two of medium length and one longer, triangular journey with two stops at other airfields. Learning the ground work was typical classroom stuff; check weather, mark route on chart, calculate compass bearings against current and predicted wind speeds and direction, and so on. I was learning to fly under visual flight rules (VFR), the most basic level, which had fairly stringent regulations about permissible visibility, cloud height and cover, and wind speeds. If any of these exceeded the limits I couldn't fly.

My first cross country solo was a simple one. Take off, turn 180 degrees, and head south at 3,000 feet following the interstate below for about twenty minutes, then touch and go on a small and unmanned rural airstrip before coming straight back home. Everything was clearly marked on the chart and no difficulties were envisaged. So I followed the route below me, which was full of traffic, and soon came to where the airstrip I was to visit was meant to be. It was there sure enough, but what I hadn't anticipated was just how tiny it was. So tiny, in fact, that on my first approach I found myself way too high (I was conditioned to land on a much bigger runway and got the time/distance relationship completely wrong) and had to go around again, which actually didn't faze me too much. Mission accomplished I followed the interstate home again and landed without further incident.

A few days later one of my friends was flying exactly the same route for his first cross country solo. He managed to land first time on the tiny airstrip because I had warned him about it. However, on his return to base he failed to notice that the wind direction had changed whilst he had been away and landed with the wind behind him rather than into it. The clubhouse emptied as his mistake became apparent and all rushed out to watch the impending disaster. He very nearly ended up landing in the woods at the end of the runway but, thankfully, managed to pull up just in time!

My second solo cross country was longer, and involved me flying to Salina (still in Kansas), where Bob told me to land, refuel, and get my logbook stamped in the control tower to prove I had actually been there. This runway was exactly the opposite of the last one, having been built for the US strategic bombers of the 1950s. I could have landed *across* the runway and still had plenty of room. I taxied across to refuel, which was a bit like filling up your car at the local petrol station, got my logbook stamped, and flew back to Leavenworth a happy chappy.

In between solos Bob took me on a flight to familiarise me with night flying, he in control at all times of course as it was way beyond my abilities and competency. We took off and after the runway lights switched off everything was dark, really dark. Bob climbed and turned and after we got level he asked me if I knew where the airstrip we had taken off from was now. I pointed, and then he did the double press on the radio send button that switched the runway lights on again and it was miles away from where I had thought it would be. I was completely discombobulated.

Anyway, he then said we'd go and have a look at Kansas City International (KCI) airport, which wasn't too far away, and soon enough we could see the lights of the runways and terminal buildings blazing in the distance. What I hadn't realised was that by 'look at' Bob had meant 'land at', but this being America I wasn't too surprised. Shortly thereafter we were being directed by KCI air traffic control to pull in behind one 747 which was about to land and look out for another 747 which was coming in behind it; we were the filling in a 747 sandwich, if you like.

Sure enough, just ahead was a jumbo jet just touching down, and a glance over my shoulder confirmed that yes, there was another one not too far behind us with landing lights blazing. We were in our little Cessna 152 in between these two giants.

You have to be careful not to hit the slipstream of a much larger aircraft if you're in a much smaller plane, for it can flip you over or otherwise severely interfere with your flight. However, Bob had obviously done this many times before and wasn't in the least bit fazed by it, and we executed a safe touch and go on the runway and returned to base. This proved not to be, however, my last adventure at KCI.

My third solo cross country flight was much longer and triangular in design, involving two stops at distant airfields and a couple of hours flying in all. The outward leg took me north into Nebraska, which if anything is even flatter than Kansas with fewer landmarks by which to navigate. Nor was I following a road this time but mainly flying on a compass bearing. So I was watching the compass closely and looking out for the various landmarks marked on the chart which would confirm I was on track.

Almost inevitably over a longer flight the wind speed and direction varied a bit, and I found myself not quite where I thought I should be. Nor was I completely sure which small town it was that I could see off to starboard in the near distance. However, I also knew that most mid-western towns had water towers for their local supply, and that the name of the town was usually emblazoned on the side of the tower. So, a quick descent down to a few hundred feet and a circuit of the water tower told me exactly where I was. Thereafter it was back up to 3,000 feet, reset the compass, and I was on my way.

The second leg took me out of Nebraska to Missouri, somewhere south east of Kansas City. It must have been uneventful because I can remember nothing about it. The final part of the triangle, however, turned out to be a bit of a saga all on its own and tested my embryonic flying skills to their very limit.

The trouble started when I was once again following a major road and check map-reading off the chart. I had set off on this solo flight a couple of hours earlier in glorious weather, but thunderstorms can blow up quickly on the prairies and dark clouds began to loom ominously ahead. It was a weather front heading directly for me, and that almost certainly meant high winds and difficult flying conditions, probably too much for a grizzled aviator to cope with let alone a student pilot like me.

The clouds got lower and lower and the wind stiffened considerably as I went ahead. Eventually, being non-instrument trained and unable to fly through the clouds, I was flying at under 1,000 feet and I knew I was going to have to land somewhere if I could to let the storm pass. I had been following the chart pretty carefully by this point, understandably, and had noticed a very small industrial airstrip just off the interstate ahead, and for want of a better solution I decided to put down there.

Despite the most atrocious crosswind landing in which I nearly, but not quite, scraped the starboard wing along the entire length of the runway, I got down in one piece, much to my immediate relief. This being America, there was of course a phone box at the edge of the tarmac, despite there being no buildings or human presence whatsoever, so I was able to call Bob back at base and explain what was going on.

All I could do was wait, and after about twenty minutes the storm had blown through and all was calm and sunshine again. I took off and headed back on my route, mindful that it was getting late in the day and that I probably shouldn't tarry any more. Whether it was because I was in a hurry or perhaps because I wasn't paying attention, I then noticed that my path was going to take me directly over Kansas City, which is a big place. I hadn't planned it that way when I filed my flight plan but it was too late in the day to do anything about it.

My memory suggests that I actually had to weave my way in between some of the radio masts which topped the skyscrapers but that can't possibly be true, can it? Do they reach up to 3,000 feet? I doubt it. Was I perhaps flying too low? A more likely explanation I fear.

Anyway, I was just leaving the city behind and below me and pleased that I was still on track when a disembodied voice crackled in my headset asking me who I was and what I was doing up there. It turned out to be KCI airport approach control and it seemed that I had inadvertently strayed into the KCI approach flight path. I replied that I was on my way to Fort Leavenworth, at which point he gave me instructions to 'squawk' on a certain frequency and turn to a new bearing. I told him, in my best Scottish/British accent, that I was afraid I didn't have a clue what he was talking about.

There was a distinct pause, then he came back with 'Are you up there alone?' I said I was. Another pause. Then he asked what aircraft I was flying. On learning it was a Cessna 152, he instructed me to look at the bottom left part of the instrument panel where there would be a transmitter and a dial with which to change its frequency. Indeed there is, I told him, and proceeded to enter the frequency he gave me and then pressed the send button. 'Ah, got you!', came the slightly triumphant call, and he then gave me a course to steer, a height at which to fly, and wished me well on my way.

Half an hour later I was back at Sherman airfield to find a mildly relieved Bob waiting for me. He reassured me that I had done most things correctly in the circumstances given my lack of experience and suggested I should go home and have a beer. This I did gladly, and I think I may have had two or three.

The next few weeks continued with further solo flights and instruction from Bob in preparation for taking my flying test with an external examiner. The weather wasn't kind and my time at Fort Leavenworth was coming rapidly to an end. I began to wonder if I'd manage to get my PPL at all after all the effort that had been put in. At the end of the course at the USACGSC I moved out of my rented house and into a local hotel for the last week of my time in the USA, and all my possessions were shipped back to the UK. It was indeed squeaky bum time, as Sir Alex Ferguson might have said.

Eventually, though, the weather cleared and I got to sit my test. I'm sure we did all the stuff I had learned – stalls, emergency landings, short take offs etc – but strangely enough the only manoeuvre I was asked to do by the examiner which sticks in my memory was a series of 360 degree banking turns without losing or gaining height. These I managed to do thanks once again to having practised them *ad nauseam* with Bob. In the end, to my immense delight and sense of achievement, I passed!

I never flew an aircraft again.

Chapter 25

Towards the end of my time at Fort Leavenworth I had begun to wonder what might lie in store for me thereafter and where my next posting might take me. Getting through to the personnel branch back in the UK wasn't easy for me as a student, so I asked the senior British officer at Fort Leavenworth if he could find out on my behalf.

This he did and a few days later he approached me with a slightly bemused expression on his face and informed me that I was being run for – that is, was on the shortlist for – the position of Military Assistant (MA) to the Deputy Supreme Allied Commander Europe (DSACEUR). Now, this was serious stuff, because that was a pretty grown up posting and usually reserved for *la crème de la crème,* so I was just as surprised as he seemed to be. As it transpired I didn't get it in the end, perhaps partially because DSACEUR at that point was General Sir John Waters, a British officer who had been Commandant at the British ASC when I had been a rather less than impressive student there. So I wasn't hugely surprised or disappointed.

It wasn't the first time in my career that I had been run for a prestigious post as it happens, for many moons previously I had been asked whether I was interested in the position of Royal Equerry to HRH The Princess of Wales, Diana herself. I didn't get that one either, and I have often wondered whether it was because the RTR wasn't considered a smart enough regiment for such a high profile role. In hindsight I'm very glad I didn't get this one, given the history of the Princess's latter days in her marriage, and I'm pretty sure it could have been disastrous for me.

Back on track. In time I was informed that my next job would be as a member of the DS at Camberley, another prestigious posting and usually a precursor to regimental command, a highly sought prize in any military officer's career. I can honestly say that I didn't really consider myself to be in that league, but others obviously thought differently. It was a huge compliment and quite unexpected. As I have already related, I hadn't exactly been a model pupil when I had attended there as a student.

So my arrival on my first day at my new job was met with a certain amount of good-humoured banter from my new colleagues, many of whom I knew already from past adventures. One trumpeted loudly to the assembled throng that my appearance on the staff was 'living proof that you *can* fool all of the people all of the time', whilst others muttered something about 'poachers turned gamekeepers' when I hove into view. That was all to be expected and expressed, and taken, in the spirit intended.

My new comrades-in-arms on the teaching staff were all bright and ambitious young lieutenant colonels on the career fast track, and some were very impressive indeed. It would be invidious to pick out individuals too much, so let me just say that I enjoyed my interactions with John Deverell of the Scots DG, Mungo Melvin of the RE, a fellow Scot who retired in the rank of Major General, and Patrick Mercer, who went on to become the Conservative MP for Newark, amongst many others.

Our job as instructors was to lead and teach our syndicates of ten younger majors or equivalents through the curriculum, which consisted of the various operations and tactics of war, including working with the other two services on joint operational planning and also with the police during the counter-terrorism module. I enjoyed the teaching part and the visits to the surrounding Surrey countryside to conduct tactical exercises, many of which remained the same from my time as a student and revolved around favoured country pubs, and which were accompanied by much waving of arms and pointing. It was ever thus.

Everybody, pupils and teachers alike, had to work pretty hard, and it was accepted that in many cases the DS were only twenty-four hours ahead of their students in terms of familiarity with the teaching material. We had some really interesting discussions and some really good central lectures from the likes of, amongst others, Ken Livingstone, the unashamedly left-wing Leader of Greater London Council at the time, and Alan Clark, former cabinet minister in Margaret Thatcher's government and author of the infamous political diaries.

It was not to last for very long as far as I was concerned, however, for after I had been teaching for a scant two terms the internal post of SO1 Planning, then occupied by my RTR friend and former HQBFME colleague Ian Rodley, fell vacant, and I was chosen to fill it. This job was essentially that of personal staff officer to the Director of Studies, who was at this time Brigadier (later Lieutenant General Sir) John Kiszely

MC, late Scots Guards. Kiszely had won his MC leading Left Flank Company of the 2nd Battalion, Scots Guards, to the top of Mount Tumbledown during the Falklands War, a particularly fierce battle in which he allegedly broke his bayonet in the body of one of the Argentinian defenders.

His military pedigree was pretty noteworthy and he had a reputation for being a bit fierce and difficult to work for, and here was I about to become his personal staff officer in the next office to his. My colleagues let out a collective sigh of relief when they learned that I had been pinged for the job, and some offered their commiserations, usually along the lines of 'rather you than me'. So I approached the position with some trepidation.

I need not have worried. Kiszely was a very easy man to work for, precise and formal at work as one would expect of a guardsman, but completely charming and relaxed away from it and in social settings. He was always kind and compassionate to me, and when I mentioned that my mother had been diagnosed with cancer he insisted that I leave work and travel back to Scotland to be with her, as it was 'much more important than anything you're doing here'. I liked him immensely and enjoyed working for him, much to my colleagues' surprise.

Another important matter that came to a head at this time was the future of the RTR. As I have already mentioned, under the terms of Options for Change, the restructuring of the British armed forces at the end of the Cold War in 1990, the four regiments (battalions) of the RTR were to reduce to two, involving the amalgamation of 1 and 4 RTR and that of 2 and 3 RTR. The immediate problem arising from this was that there were at the time four RTR lieutenant colonels – Ian Rodley, John Lemon, David Eccles, and me – all of whom ordinarily would have had the reasonable expectation of commanding one of the RTRs. Now it appeared that our prospects had been cut by fifty per cent.

I realised this early on in the process and had already carried out my own personal evaluation. Ian Rodley was an exact contemporary of mine but had been promoted to lieutenant colonel a year earlier than me, while John Lemon and David Eccles were younger than me but we had been promoted at the same time. It seemed logical to me, therefore, that I was number four, at the bottom of the list. At the same time, the imminent disappearance of 4 RTR from the British army order of battle changed everything as far as I was concerned. If I were, contrary to my calculations, chosen to command one of the two remaining RTRs after the amalgamations it just wouldn't be the same.

RHQ RTR should have sorted all of this out beforehand, of course, but it was typically slow off the mark. The regiment's future plan for command, or the command plot as it was called, was known only to a few and guarded with some secrecy. Information was, and is, power, and we were expected to wait until such times as it was deemed appropriate for us to be told of our fate. Regimental command was regarded as the apogee of a regimental career and accordingly we should be grateful to wait until we were told it was to be ours, or so it seemed to me.

Well, I wasn't having any of this. Working on the premise that nobody had informed me that I was likely to command and that I had worked out, rightly or wrongly, that I was the least likely one to get it, I decided to take my future in my own hands and inform RHQ RTR that I didn't want to do it anyway.

Much of this was settled, not at RHQ RTR as you might think, but at an informal meeting held in the staff college in Camberley when all four of us just happened to be there at the same time. That is when I basically told the others that I was out, and no more was said about it amongst us. I did, however, then have to relay my decision via the RAC personnel and manning branch, where it was met with a certain amount of dismay and disbelief.

There then followed a succession of phone calls to me from officers of ever-ascending rank until finally the Representative Colonel Commandant of the RTR himself, General Sir Antony Walker, rang me to ask if, amongst other things, I was really serious about this. I explained to him, politely but firmly, that keeping prospective commanding officers completely in the dark about their future or potential appointments was particularly poor man management, in my opinion, and both demeaning and insulting to those concerned. And, yes, I was serious, so that was that.

The consensus amongst my contacts across many other regiments was that my case had been very badly handled indeed by the RTR, especially when it transpired that I *was* in line for command. I never had any regrets, however, not even when I attended as a guest at the amalgamation parade of 1 and 4 RTR at Tidworth on Salisbury Plain later in 1993. If the truth be told, it signified a takeover by 4 RTR, especially in the sergeants' mess where we were very strong, and also with the pipes and drums, the regimental tartan, and the

Chinese Eyes on the tanks all being carried forward into the new, amalgamated regiment.

As for me, I viewed the parade and subsequent festivities as a kind of dispassionate bystander, for what I had held most dear had now gone. I enjoyed the company of the officers and soldiers still serving whom I knew and recognised, then went home without a backwards glance. I had made my own bed, as it were, and was content to lie in it.

Chapter 26

Having unwittingly taken a wrecking ball to the RTR command plot, the question then arose of what I was going to do post-Camberley. Most DS tours there lasted no longer than two and a half years, and my time was nearly up. Whilst I had enjoyed my time there it was time to move on, but there was no obvious career posting open to me at that point.

However, I had long harboured an ambition to undertake a Defence Fellowship (DF). At that time in the mid-1990s, two officers from all three services would be awarded a DF to study at a university of their choice a topic of mutual interest to both them and the military, producing a report to the MoD at the end of their year in academia. It might, or might not, be accompanied by the award of an academic qualification from the university itself, depending on the quality and relevance of the work carried out.

The scheme was competitive and completely self-initiated and voluntary. Those who aspired to a DF had to identify an area of study they thought was relevant, in pretty broad terms to be fair, to their employer, argue the case for why they should be permitted to carry it out, and submit their proposal to the

MoD for official approval and confirmation. The guidelines were vague, probably deliberately so.

I have never really considered myself much of an academic but I had enjoyed my various brushes with academia, and had spent more time than most of my peer group in quasi academic institutions like the two staff colleges I had attended both as student and instructor. I did think, therefore, that a DF might be right up my street if I was lucky enough to secure one. The immediate questions confronting me were what topic to research and where to study it.

After a bit of thought and deliberation, it struck me that the thorny topic of race relations was a bit of a hot potato at the time in British military circles, as indeed it still is today. A modicum of background research showed that there had already been quite a few studies into the difficulties of recruiting into all three services from Britain's visible ethnic communities, which at that time (1994) made up roughly seven per cent of the UK population but only 1.4 per cent of the regular British armed services, with the proportion of officers significantly lower at 0.9 per cent.

Perhaps more significant was the fact that in the sixteen to twenty-four age bracket, the traditional recruiting ground for the services, those minorities then accounted for sixteen per cent of the population. While there might have been longstanding historical and cultural reasons for their lack of more proportional representation, I wondered if what happened *within* the armed services had any part to play in it. It seemed to me an interesting area to investigate.

As to where I might try to research and study the topic, the traditional locations to undertake Defence Fellowships tended to be King's College, London, or Cambridge University. Well, I had already attended the latter as an undergraduate and I had no desire to be in London; nice place to visit for a couple of days *de temps en temps* but death if I had to be there permanently. At the same time, I had a hankering to return to Scotland, and for two main reasons.

The first and most important was that my folks, who lived just outside Glasgow, were getting on a bit and I'd been away for a while and therefore I was keen to spend a bit more time with them, especially after my mother had just beaten her first bout of 'the cancer', as they might put it back home. My sister's children were also growing up fast too and I wanted to get to know them better.

On top of this, my nascent interest in all things political had been exacerbated by the debate on the possibility of Scottish independence. I had long been a bit of a Scottish nationalist (with a small 'n') and it looked to me like the next few years might be very interesting indeed in terms of Scottish politics. So, putting those factors together, I decided to see if Glasgow University might be prepared to take me on.

Now, it just so happened that the *well-kent* historian Hew Strachan – now Professor Sir Hew Strachan – had just set up the Scottish Centre for War Studies at the University and, after a short telephone discussion, said he was happy to host me for the first part of my research and also to be my academic supervisor, which was a bit of an early coup. Thereafter my study would be heading more into social studies territory, and

I was pleased that the Department for Social and Economic Research was prepared to accommodate me too.

With agreement in principle from all the relevant parties I submitted my application to the MoD and, lo and behold, it came to pass that I was awarded my DF. I then moved from Camberley to Glasgow, a complete lock, stock, and barrel 'flitting' as we are wont to say in these parts, and was allocated a tied military house (MQ) in the suburb of Thornliebank. I knew the area passing well as it wasn't far from my old school's playing fields where I had been an appallingly poor rugby player many years before.

It was also about ten minutes' drive away from my boyhood home where my parents lived for over fifty years and close to my sister too. To get into the university I had only to walk a short distance to the local rail station to catch the train, then transfer to the very wonderful Glasgow subway – never the Tube – from St Enoch's Square to Byres Road, then walk up the hill to the department. I was only a hop, skip, and jump away from the university army careers office where I had taken my first tentative steps into the army some fifteen years previously.

I loved being back in Glasgow. The city has many attributes, of course, but I had forgotten just how fine much of the architecture is. It is often said that Glasgow is one of the most physically attractive cities in Europe if you look upwards, and after many years away and having visited many places I tended to agree. I also relished hearing once more the banter and repartee of my fellow 'Weegies', which had been so prevalent when I had been with my regiment.

Everybody talks to everybody else in Glasgow and you're never alone. In fact, you can always guarantee getting involved in a conversation even if you don't want to! The contrast with Edinburgh and London, where everyone tends to keep themselves to themselves, is very noticeable. There is also a bit of an edge to the city. Whilst the days of the street-fighting gangs of *No Mean City* are long gone, well mostly anyway, there is still more than enough crime that spills out of the vast peripheral housing schemes to keep the authorities busy.

Personally I have never experienced any real trouble or bother while going about my everyday business both as boy and man there, but I was always conscious of where not to go, especially after dark. It was second nature to avoid certain areas with fearsome reputations, but even then I have to say that in my youth I had been in some of the roughest, toughest parts and been met only with friendly banter and kindness, often from the poorest of the poor.

Anyway, I started my year at the university in eager anticipation. Being back in that environment again after twenty years or so was a revelation in terms of how I had misspent my undergraduate years. Youth is truly wasted on the young. I couldn't believe my luck at having a full access to the splendid library, a free hand to study my chosen subject, and all the while be free from the usual financial worries of most students because I was still on a full lieutenant colonel's salary, with legitimate travel and other expenses to boot, whilst the MoD kindly picked up my tuition fees.

Mind you, I did have to work. I had split my study into three broad sections; the first was to be an historical overview of the employment of ethnic and racial groups in the British army; the second was to be a comparative look at how other large institutions, overseas militaries, police forces, public and private organisations, dealt with their problems, if any; and the third part was to encompass original qualitative and quantitative research into what was going on inside the British army at that time.

The historical part I carried out under the expert guidance of Hew Strachan. I wanted to look at how the army had used its distinctly different races and ethnic groups throughout history, although I quickly realised I could only hope to scratch the surface of such a vast topic. However I felt it an important backdrop to the main thrust of my thesis. The first historical example I chose was the integration of Scots into what was to become the British army, which happened in two main tranches; that which happened between the Union of the Crowns in 1603 and the Union of the Parliaments in 1707, and the absorption of the Jacobite highlanders in the aftermath of the 1745 rebellion.

The latter case is perhaps more interesting, and I discovered that a number of factors seem to have been at play here. Some were overtly political, like the desire to remove a source of political instability overseas as quickly as possible, in this case to America to fight the French. Another was economic, as in the desire of Highland Jacobite chiefs to be reintegrated into the British ruling classes and hopefully regain their forfeited lands in the process. Another factor might have been the wish to integrate the former Jacobite soldiery into British society by the rite of passage of military service, although we mustn't try to be clever here with the benefit of hindsight.

I found similar themes when I came to examine Britain's use of Indian troops in the sepoy companies of the East India Company and later in the Indian army of the Empire. Here the challenges presented made it imperative that troops were raised locally to help police it; British troops could not hope to do it alone. Plus native troops were cheaper too, with their pay on average less than half that of the equivalent British rank. In addition, British troops were a wasting asset, losing far more soldiers to disease than to battle. The proportion of British soldiers to Indian varied from as few as one in eight before the Indian Mutiny of 1857 to roughly one in two thereafter, but the military task would have been quite simply impossible without Indian troops.

The third historical example I looked at was perhaps the most interesting of all, involving the raising of West Indian soldiers for service against the French in the Caribbean in the aftermath of the French Revolution of 1789. Here the use of native troops had an added dimension, for the vast majority of black West Indians 'recruited' were in fact slaves. Indeed, many of these slave-soldiers were bought straight off the slave ships, and in 1806 and 1807 – despite the Slave Trade Act of that latter year – slaving companies were actually commissioned by the British government to provide slaves for its army.

Yet once again the main driving force behind the recruitment of local troops was the need for military manpower. And the primary reason for this, although there were many others, was the reality of military service in the West Indies itself. It was considered a death sentence by those white troops sent out to garrison the islands, and a glance at the statistics tells you why.

Some 43,750 white NCOs and men died either in the Caribbean or en route between 1793 and 1801, nearly fifty-one per cent of those serving there when the conflict began, plus a further 1,500 officers who suffered the same fate.

In contrast, black and Creole slaves were available in numbers, acclimatised, and immune to the endemic yellow fever which destroyed so many British regiments. They were also not addicted to the raw cane rum which predisposed British soldiers to the ravages of the disease, and also had a better diet. Consequently, their mortality rate was about thirty per cent of that of British and European troops in the period 1796-1816.

However, it was not all one-way exploitation of black slave labour by the military, no matter what modern 'woke' historians might have you believe otherwise. Whilst slavery was of course a great evil, the slave-soldiers lot was considerably better than that of their plantation brethren. The black soldiers were treated in the same hospitals, wore the same uniforms, and enjoyed the same pay, allowances, and privileges as their white comrades-in-arms.

But the most fundamental advantage that service in the British West Indian Army, and also in other European colonial armies in the Caribbean at that time, gave the slave-soldier was that it gained him his freedom. It became normal practice to give the black 'recruits' their freedom after five years' service with the colours. This fact has not found general acceptance with a certain genre of modern historians, it has to be said, but I report here what I found at the time.

I could recount many other historical examples and interesting lessons, but they're all in my 40,000-word report I forwarded to the MoD at the end of my DF and which I doubt anybody there has ever read. There is a copy, however, in the House of Lords library, and I'll relate how it got there later.

The next part of my plan, the comparison with other organisations, followed. This involved a bit of travelling, quite a lot of travelling in one particular instance, which I was able to do because the MoD kindly provided me with a travel budget for research purposes. After some thought, I settled on having a look at how the Australian Defence Forces (ADF), Greater Manchester and Strathclyde police forces, and British Gas designed and implemented their policies.

I chose the ADF because it had its origins firmly rooted in the British military tradition and was accordingly more directly comparable than, say, the US army. The ADF had also just carried out a major and comprehensive investigation into its ethnic composition which was to be a rich source of information on its attitudes and practices. And, if we're being totally honest here, I had never been to Australia and quite fancied going there to take a look, especially as I could tack on my annual leave at the end of my study visit and have a bit of a holiday.

So off I went. I won't bore you with the details of the outward journey except to say it was long and as unglamorous as modern air travel can be. Once in Australia I made my way to Canberra, where luckily an Aussie officer who had been at the staff college at Camberley with me happened to be. He was able to furnish me with an abundance of material which was pertinent to my research, and I retreated to Sydney and Melbourne to digest it while seeing a bit of the country at the same time.

What did I think of Australia? Well, to be honest, I was a bit underwhelmed. Sydney was nice in the centre, and the suburbs of Melbourne reminded me of Giffnock in Glasgow only warmer, and some of the bits of the countryside in New South Wales were nice. But lots of it looked a bit arid, featureless, and ramshackle to my European eyes, although to be fair my travels inside the country were not that extensive.

The Australians I met I liked, as I had always done with their diaspora in the UK, finding them kind and amusing. Some of them were a bit too 'hail fellow, well met' for my personal taste, but that probably says more about me than it does them. No harm done. I was happy to get back to the UK, though, and continue with my other visits there.

The police provided another suitable subject for comparison. Like the armed services they are a uniformed, disciplined organisation with a hierarchical structure, form an important pillar of the state, and have codes of practice and discipline which set them apart from much of the rest of society. I visited both Greater Manchester Police (GMP) and Strathclyde Police (SP), and though I can't remember much about either visit they provided a lot of material for me to consider.

In particular, both forces were keen to reflect as closely as possible the communities they were responsible for policing, and whilst they both deemed their respective situations as unsatisfactory at that time, they had policies in place to address the imbalances in ethnic minority representation in their ranks. They were quite a bit ahead of the army, I thought, and there was a lot to learn from them.

My final visit was to British Gas to look at how a large civilian commercial organisation in the industrial sector approached race and ethnicity matters. I found that in many ways they were ahead of all the other civilian organisations I had visited with a comprehensive system of ethnic monitoring in place in accordance with Commission for Racial Equality (CRE) guidelines at that time. They also had arguably the best complaints and redress of grievance that I had discovered, which gave me plenty food for thought.

The final part of my study involved looking at the British army itself and finding out what was actually going on. This was to be done first by promulgating a questionnaire I had designed and drafted under the supervision of my academic advisers. It was then distributed to a random, stratified sample of 1,600 army personnel and achieved a return rate of just shy of fifty-two per cent. Everybody seemed to think that this was pretty good given the anonymous and voluntary nature of the survey, and I passed on the detailed results to the MoD for further analysis after extracting the gist of the answers.

The macro results of the questionnaire seemed to indicate three things; the first was that, despite official denials at the time, there was widespread racial discrimination in the army; second, only a small proportion of those who indicated that they had suffered racial discrimination had ever complained or made representations via the army's internal grievance procedures, mainly because they thought it would adversely affect their careers; and thirdly, just over one half of those who did complain – albeit a small sample – were satisfied with the outcome.

To allow an initial qualitative cross-check on the results of the questionnaire it was decided to hold a series of interviews and focus groups with serving personnel, with the permission of the MoD of course. Initially I had intended to do these myself, but wiser counsel persuaded me that my rank would be off-putting for junior soldiers and they might feel constrained and unable to answer without fear or favour. Consequently they were carried out by my supervisor and mentor in social science research, John Money, a thoroughly nice chap who used to smile wryly at my decidedly military approach to things.

These interviews confirmed much of what the questionnaire had already suggested. There was clearly a major problem with racial discrimination within the army, which interviewees said was obviously having a detrimental effect on recruiting and retention amongst the ethnic minorities and that there was little faith in redress of grievance procedures, which followed the chain of command. This was primarily because, in many cases, the person to whom a complainant would have to apply for redress would be the very same person who was perpetrating the perceived discrimination in the first place!

I also carried out a number of other interviews with other bodies and individuals during the course of my year's study, including most notably with the CRE itself and with the politicians Menzies Campbell MP and Dr John Reid MP. Mr Campbell I met at the House of Commons where he kindly hosted me, whilst Dr Reid, who was the Labour party spokesman on defence then and later Secretary of State for Defence when Labour came to power, I ambushed at one of his constituency surgeries in Motherwell. This particular interview led to interesting events which I will return to later.

In the end I typed it all up and produced my 40,000 word report which I sent off to the MoD. I made a number of recommendations, but the three most important ones, I think, were: that the army needed to implement a comprehensive and transparent methodology for ethnic monitoring to fully understand the problems it faced; that the redress of grievance procedure was not fit for purpose and needed to be replaced by one that operated independently of the chain of command, and that an equal opportunities ombudsman should be appointed, again independent of the chain of command, to oversee the processes involved.

I heard nothing from the MoD after the submission of my report as I had rather suspected would be the case, because its contents and recommendations would not have been particularly welcome. Sensing that this might be the case and that it might be buried by the powers that be, I took the decision to follow academic practice and send a copy to all the organisations and individuals I had consulted in the hope that somebody might read it and take it seriously.

It was this decision which was to come back to bite me a few months later.

Chapter 27

Having completed my DF, and having vandalised the career path that others had chosen for me without consulting me first, I found myself at a bit of a loose end.

By this time it had been decided, however, by whoever it was that decided such things, that my command appointment would be as the City of Edinburgh Universities Officer Training Corps (CEUOTC), well down the pecking order of command appointments, below regular and TA commands, training establishment commands, depot and weapons development commands, right on the bottom layer if you like, and hardly what I would have once aspired to, but there you have it. I had ploughed my own furrow and could hardly complain at the result.

What I *had* hoped for was command of the Scottish Yeomanry (SY), a TA unit of the RAC headquartered in Edinburgh with sub units scattered across Scotland, but it was not to be. Apparently it was 'the turn of the TA' to nominate an officer to take over there, which was an interesting way of determining such appointments, although I can just about understand the rationale in a peacetime army. Although one must ask, what would have happened if we had gone to war? But no sour grapes from me, either at the time or now. However, the OTC was a complete mystery to me as I had not joined mine when I was at university. More of this later.

In terms of timing, though, the end of my spell at Glasgow University did not conform to the army's command plot, and I had roughly eight months to spare. Luckily for me, this hiatus in my military employment was spotted by the General Officer Commanding Scotland (GOC Scotland), Major General Jonny Hall, late of the Scots DG, and he pinched me to work for him at Army HQ Scotland which was located in Craigiehall, just to the west of Edinburgh. So I upped sticks from Glasgow and moved to the capital.

General Hall had been commander of 12 Armd Bde in Germany of which 4 RTR had been part during my last stint in Osnabruck, so essentially I had been one of his tank squadron leaders. He thought kindly of me, and I of him, so I was very pleased to take up a temporary post in his HQ and renew our acquaintance. He had created a new post for me, that of SO1 Image, which meant that I was the lieutenant colonel in charge of public relations and media communications, which suited me down to the ground. I had been the PR officer for 4 RTR for a time, and had long had an interest in writing and photography. At staff college I had written for, and edited, both the official and unofficial magazine and scurrilous news-sheet, had written and reviewed books for the regimental magazine, and had also penned a few more serious pieces for the British Army Review (BAR), the in-house journal of the army.

At the same time I thoroughly enjoyed the company of journalists, who seemed to occupy one of the last bastions of excess, both at work and play, and whose companionship in both reminded me of some of the best times I had spent as a young officer back in the day. They were funny and irreverent to a fault and provided just the right environment for me to operate in my new role.

I could name many of them, but I had particularly close ties with Ian Bruce, who worked for the Glasgow Herald and who was the only proper defence correspondent working in the Scottish media at the time. Our paths had crossed many times in the past, including in Cyprus and the Gulf, and it was just great to be able to spend more time with him, often in the company of the late, great Clive Fairweather, formerly of the SAS and later Her Majesty's Inspector of Prisons for Scotland. We had some riotous times I can tell you, and our midweek lunches are the stuff of legend. Many of these were spent in the Doric, Scotland's oldest gastropub close to Waverley Station in Edinburgh, which was ideal for Ian to get back to Glasgow without having to walk too far!

The general's instruction to me on taking up my position was a classic example of brevity, simplicity, and mission-orientated orders; he said he wanted me to take the army back into Scottish society, having become concerned that we were becoming increasingly isolated from the very communities from which we drew our recruits. He told me what he wanted done, not how I was to do it, which is the essence of *auftragstaktik,* where the emphasis is on the outcome of a mission rather than the specific means of achieving it. I was given a free hand, basically and set about my task from first principles.

The first thing I tried to do was to get the army more frequent and prominent coverage in the Scottish media, primarily the newspapers. This was not difficult, given that I knew a number of journalists already. Arranging to meet them individually and brief them on the army's presence and purpose in Scotland was pure pleasure. What I had not expected, though, was how the press ran the various stories that appeared. Rather than concentrating, initially at least, on the message we were trying to put over, they chose to write about my appointment – not about me *per se*, but about the new post the army had instituted.

These stories were usually accompanied by photographs of me, which I found amusing, but some of the old and stuffy retired officer types who now worked in a civilian capacity in the HQ, the classic Bufton Tuftons as *Private Eye* might put it, got decidedly sniffy about it all and started looking askance and muttering under their breath whenever I passed by their desks. They must have thought, quite wrongly I can say, that I was on a massive ego trip and lapping up all the coverage, but nothing could be further from the truth. I was just doing the job I had been asked to do, so Hell mend them I thought.

The other thing I started which caused much less irritation, thankfully, was a new in-house journal which came to be called MASCOT (magazine of the Army in Scotland – clever, eh?). I hoped it would not only become another means of internal communications with all the military units in Scotland but also might penetrate that bit of civilian society which had an interest in military matters. My first couple of attempts at magazine production, aided by our in-house media team and others who had a modicum of publishing experience, were admittedly a bit amateurish. Not quite cut and paste as in glue and scissors, but only a couple of steps on from that. Happily the magazine fell into more accomplished hands after I left and is still going strong today I understand. It is now a much more professional and presentable product and on a par with other commercial magazines and journals.

In parallel with this activity, General Jonny signed me up to participate in the Edinburgh Common Purpose programme. I had no idea what it was but was happy to get involved. It was billed as a programme of events and seminars for 'the leaders of tomorrow', which caused me much merriment, and ran through the year, taking us on educational and insightful visits to all sorts of organisations involved in government, education, the arts, health, justice, and charities amongst others. The details escape me now, but one memorable visit was made to Saughton Prison in Edinburgh, where we found ourselves sitting around a table chatting away to long term prisoners, including a couple of double murderers, about their lives and experiences. Interestingly, we all thought they were terribly nice!

Common Purpose describes itself as 'a global leadership organisation devoted to developing leaders who can cross boundaries. Both at work and in society', and I was happy to take that at face value. Others have been more suspicious of its real purpose, likening it to a cult or something akin to a secret society spreading its tentacles around the world. I suspect this is just the usual conspiracy theory nonsense that seems to be all pervasive these days, but I retain a mind open to be persuaded otherwise. All I can say is that I found it most educational at the time but have had virtually no contact with the organisation since.

Occasionally I got roped into other duties as part of the HQ staff. One of the more enjoyable ones was assisting with the hosting of the general's guests at the Edinburgh Military Tattoo, held every year over a period of weeks during the Edinburgh International Festival. I was involved in this on numerous occasions, but perhaps the most memorable one was when the guest of honour was the Secretary of State for Defence at the time, Michael Portillo.

The pre-Tattoo reception was held at the general's house at Gogarburn, just outside Edinburgh proper, where we had drinks and dinner. Portillo, who didn't always have the best press, turned out to be rather charming – so the ladies seemed to think anyway – and an amusing *raconteur* and conversationalist. Then, at the appointed time, we were loaded into a convoy of staff cars and minibuses and driven to Edinburgh Castle with a full escort of police cars and motorcycle outriders. It's the only time I have ever experienced this sort of VIP treatment, with all other traffic stopped and being given priority passage at traffic lights and junctions, and I must admit I got a great amount of childish pleasure from it.

At the Tattoo itself Portillo took the salute, standing up alone in the VIP stand, which I thought was rather brave of him given the unpopularity of his party and government in Scotland when Mrs Thatcher was Prime Minister. However, to everybody else's relief, no rotten fruit or bricks were thrown at him, although I did hear a few boos from the crowd.

Looking back on it all I must admit that the short time I spent at Army HQ Scotland was very pleasant indeed. I lived on the army 'patch' in Colinton in Edinburgh and commuted the short distance to Craigiehall every day in the rather battered third-hand VW Polo I bought for just that purpose. The office building where we all worked was classic cheap, 1960s disaster utilitarian architecture at its worst, but the officers' mess was in a large, traditional baronial style Scottish country house which did a passing good lunch.

Sadly the status of Army HQ Scotland has since diminished over the years, including a short hiatus when there was no GOC Scotland at all, until the HQ was merged with the HQ of 51 Infantry Bde in Stirling. Craigiehall no more, as the Proclaimers might have put it.

Chapter 28

The time came for me to leave Army HQ Scotland and take over command at the CEUOTC. OTCs had their origins back at the beginning of the nineteenth century, when the Secretary of State for War, Lord Haldane, appointed a committee to address the problem of a shortage of officers in the reserve forces. The committee recommended that an Officers' Training Corps be formed in two divisions: the junior division in public schools and the senior division in the universities.

In 1908 the OTCs came into being, just in time for the First World War for which they provided over 20,500 officers. CEUOTC had its origins much earlier in history, however, in No. 4 Company of the 1st City of Edinburgh Rifle Volunteer Corps which was raised in 1859. Some ninety volunteers from the University of Edinburgh went on to join the company. When Haldane instituted the OTCs in 1908 he was actually Rector of the University of Edinburgh at the time. Some 2,250 students from the university were commissioned during the First World War.

The purpose of the UOTCs was, and is, to develop the leadership abilities of their members alongside giving them a taste of military life whilst at university. They also organise non-military outdoor pursuits as part of their programme, including adventurous pursuits and sports. Equally important to the young people who join them, I suspect, is the buoyant social life they promote, with cheap alcohol in the bar, and the fact that the students get paid for their attendance. What's not to like?

The British army's official line is a bit more po-faced: 'University students who join the University Officers' Training Corps will have the opportunity to undertake Reserve Officer training modules designed to fit around their degrees. This will teach you everything from how to wear a uniform correctly to the ability to lead others in stressful situations. The UOTC provides a standard of experience and training that is well respected within the army, and highly sought after by numerous civilian employers. The UOTC also develops leadership through Sport and Adventurous Training. Each unit has teams for most major sports and in Adventurous Training, you can experience everything from kayaking to rock climbing.'

When I looked at it after a few weeks settling in it seemed to me that the UOTC in Edinburgh had two main purposes. The first was to provide youngsters at the local universities with a social club in uniform, if you like, which might or might not persuade them that a stint in the regular army post-graduation might be worth a shot. There was absolutely no compulsion on them to join the armed services after university and most of them did not, which was fine. The positive PR that the army got from this high-achieving cadre of graduates was more than worth the effort, and I couldn't see anything wrong with regarding it as an army themed university club run along more or less the same lines as any other university society.

Its second main function, I thought, was to provide junior officers for the TA, and here the CEUOTC seemed to have taken its eye off the ball over the years. The number of OTC members who had been commissioned into the TA in the years previous to my command was abysmally small, and so, after a time assessing the options, I took that as my main mission whilst I was there. I was going to try to increase dramatically the number of commissions we would achieve, and in this we were ultimately successful, I'm pleased to say. In the second year of my tenure we managed to produce no fewer than fifteen junior officers for the TA, of which I think the CEUOTC could be justifiably proud.

This was not a solo effort, of course, and I was hugely assisted and supported by my 2ic Steve Bargeton, a TA officer in the Black Watch who was also a journalist in the Dundee Courier, two very capable RSMs and other NCO instructors, plus some other younger officers who came and went as their parallel civilian careers allowed. My sole previous experience at unit level, if you like, had been with the first class frontline armoured regiment that was 4th Tanks, thus the UOTC took a bit of getting used to initially.

The biggest difference, obviously, was that the OTC was a part time unit which programmed its activities around the cadets' academic commitments. It had no operational remit whatsoever except some residual responsibilities should the UK ever again enter a war of national survival, which was, and still is, very unlikely. Plus all of my soldiers were by definition potential officer material and there were absolutely no disciplinary problems, not that I was aware of anyway.

Compared to a regular regiment the routine was simple. The students turned up on designated drill nights during the week and every other weekend. The nights started with a quick muster parade and then they dispersed into groups under their various instructors to learn the basic military skills – map-reading, skill-at-arms, first aid and so on. After a couple of hours or so we would call it a day and the students invariably adjourned to the bar, which I think stayed open until the last person decided to go home.

We did venture out on exercise too, and I became familiar with assorted small training areas in Scotland, including the Pentland Hills just outside Edinburgh and the Barry Buddon training area in Angus, near Carnoustie and its famous Open Championship golf course. Here we did some low level tactical instruction and used the ranges for live firing. On other occasions we went farther afield, like when our RE troop got involved in a project on Islay in the Inner Hebrides, ancient seat of the Lord of the Isles, helping with some restoration work at their historic capital at Finlaggan.

To be honest, such forays tended to be self-contained at NCO instructor level and there was not that much for me to do save make what I always called my 'morale shattering visits' to the troops in the field. I did enjoy, though, the journey by army helicopter from Edinburgh to Islay, one of the perks of the job, which was conducted at a sensibly low level that let me see central Scotland from the air as I had never seen it before.

The OTC was headquartered in Duke of Edinburgh House in Colinton, in a compound shared with other minor units. By great good fortune the SY was right next door, and one of my closest and oldest friend from 4th Tanks, Charlie Pelling, had just been appointed their training major, so there were lots of mutual visits paid. Charlie had joined 4 RTR on the very same day as me way back in 1980, had been best man at my wedding, and is godfather to my elder daughter, so he and I know each other well.

All in all it was a pretty relaxed existence, cushy even. There was only one fly in the ointment, but sadly a big one. CEUOTC came under the administrative control – not command for we were not an operational unit – of HQ 52 Bde which was located in Edinburgh Castle itself. And the commander of 52 Bde was a thoroughly nasty piece of work. Grossly overweight, red of face and bad-tempered to a fault, he was the only superior officer I even came close to having a confrontation with in all my twenty years in the army.

I had met him once before, on Exercise Lionheart in Germany in 1984, when the regiment supported the battalion he was commanding (poor souls!) in a river crossing exercise. Neither my CO nor I had thought much of him at the time, and on our next meeting I didn't see much to make me change my mind. If anything he had simply become even nastier.

Now, 52 Bde was a pretty third tier brigadier appointment, and probably not the operational brigade appointment that our man had been hoping for, so I guess he must have been a tad disappointed. So, being thwarted in his ambition and of limited intellect by nature, he did what that possibly apocryphal French general in the Franco-Prussian War did when he abandoned his troops in the front line and busied himself straightening the tent lines in the rear: he retreated into his comfort zone. And his comfort zone was administration.

In effect he became the brigade administrator rather than the brigade commander. Now, I'll be the first to admit that the CEUOTC's internal administration wasn't our strong point, nor had it been for many years. Everything was in its place, though, and there wasn't even a hint of malpractice or corruption in any of the accounts, but when our annual review of the unit indicated that we weren't exactly top of the tree in recording everything properly, the brigadier pounced like a bird of prey. I was summoned to Edinburgh Castle and basically told I had to sack my admin officer.

What the brigadier hadn't expected, perhaps, was for me to refuse point blank to do so. It was my command, modest though it may have been, and I was damned if it was going to be micromanaged by anyone above me in the chain of command. If our admin was found wanting then I'd sort it out. That's what the current army doctrinal paradigm of mission orders was all about, after all; tell 'em what you want done, but don't tell 'em how to do it. Or, as General Rupert Smith who commanded 1 (UK) Armd Div in the Gulf might have put it more succinctly, direct and then let them get on with it. That's what a confident commander should do.

The brigadier wasn't in the same league as Smith, in fact his name shouldn't be mentioned in the same breath, so he seized on the inspection report as an excuse to send in his own inspection team, which was designed as both a huge insult to

me and my unit and a blatant attempt to bully me to bend to
his will. But I was having none of it, and although my annual
confidential report that year was by far the worst of my military
career, I won by being stubborn. My admin officer stayed. Our
esteemed commander had made the classic mistake of confusing
purpose with process, and was more interested with how our
books looked than our output of young officers into the TA.

What goes around comes around, though, and years later
when both Charlie P and I had left the colours and shared an
office in Hanover Street in Edinburgh as we sought to make our
way in civvy street, news came which cheered us no end. Long
after he had tormented us in 52 Bde, our unpleasant brigadier
was sent off to some far flung corner of the former Empire as
a defence attache (DA). There he fell for the sultry charms of
some *femme fatale* who just happened to be working for the local
security and intelligence services in a classic honeypot sting.

Hopelessly compromised when this came to light and at risk
of blackmail, he was despatched home with his tail between his
legs. To say a shiver of *schadenfreude* ran through us would be
a complete understatement, more an orgiastic convulsion of
pleasure at his downfall. We made sure that the Scottish media
got all the detail they were looking for, in particular ensuring
they knew his nickname of 'the tartan barrel', on account of his
immense girth, made the papers, which it duly did. Game, set,
and match to us, don't you think?

There were other perks that came with being a CO in
Edinburgh. I was made an honorary member of the Royal Scots
Club. Although not really a clubbable sort of person I rather
liked it; it was convenient, it was generally quiet, and it had an

all ranks membership and was not just for officers as so many military clubs seem to be. The club is in fact a war memorial, set up instead of the usual regimental monuments to honour the 11,162 members of the Royal Scots battalions who had been killed in the First World War.

Over the years, as those who had fought with the Royal Scots in both world wars dwindled, membership had been opened up to family members, then anyone who had served in the armed services, and finally to anyone duly proposed by a member and accepted. It was a nice place and I used to do some of my military business there, and continued to use it for a while when I returned to civvy street. I haven't been there recently and I may still be a member, although I haven't asked. At least I haven't been kicked out as far as I am aware!

Another perk was being able to have my younger daughter christened at St Margaret's Chapel inside Edinburgh Castle. Reputedly the oldest surviving building in the capital, it was built in the twelfth century and named after Margaret, a pious English princess of the House of Wessex who died in the Castle in 1093 and was canonized in 1250. The chapel is approximately ten feet wide by twenty feet long and so is not very big at all. In this tiny space it was possible, as I was serving in Scotland, for me to hold the baptism with a small number of guests. We were given exclusive use of the chapel, which is usually a favourite for tourists, during the duration of the service.

What made it even nicer was that my mother, who was getting on a bit and had just seen off her cancer for the second time, was given special permission – without me asking – to drive in her car across the drawbridge and all the way up the winding, climbing road through the castle to right outside the chapel, a rare privilege. And, to round the whole event off, as we emerged after the christening, coachloads of Japanese tourists were waiting outside who, thinking that we might be very special people if not minor Scottish celebrities, unleashed a barrage of flashbulbs as they took photographs of us all leaving. What a hoot!

There were more serious matters too. One day whilst sitting at my desk and contemplating the ways of the world my phone rang, as it did sometimes. The disembodied voice of an anonymous caller from the MoD in London informed me that someone would be calling in to see me the next day. When I enquired who they might be and what they might want I was told that all would be made clear when they arrived. I then knew straight away what it would be. The security services have long recognised Britain's university campuses as fertile recruiting grounds for new operatives, and the UOTCs offer a reasonably secure and trusted entry for such talent spotting. Indeed, academia has long been a stamping ground for such activities.

And so it was. A fit looking, tanned young man presented himself in my office the next day, came in and sat down, and without further ado announced that he was from the Secret Intelligence Service (SIS) and that he was interested to know whether I'd be up for doing some talent spotting for them. At that point in the conversation I mentioned the names of a couple of friends of mine who I knew worked in his organisation which took him aback momentarily. I mean, it's meant to be secret, isn't it?

However, after a brief chat I said I'd be happy to help as it seemed to me to be a good thing to do, so he handed me over his card with phone number and took his leave. I can't remember the name on the card but it was almost certainly a *nom de guerre,* but over the next few months we spoke occasionally and I interviewed and recommended a few of my cadets, mainly female as it happens, to him. I have no idea if any of them took it any further, or if any of them ended up in MI6, but that was the nature of the beast. The last time I called his number, after my political affiliations became wider known, it had been disconnected.

Of much more serious concern to me, however, was another set of events which began similarly. Once again I was sitting at my desk in my office, and once again the phone rang, and once again a disembodied and anonymous voice from the MoD was on the line. This time, however, the caller had a question: 'Are you aware that your DF report is currently being debated in the House of Lords?' was the question. I was not, I replied, whilst thinking to myself how can it possibly have ended up there? The caller had little more to say, but I could tell by his tone that he thought it was all a bit of a rum deal.

If we're being honest here, which I like to think I am, I had always hoped that my work wouldn't just disappear into the black hole that is the MoD and die a lonely death just because those who decided such things, whomsoever they might have been, didn't like what I had found out about racism in the army nor the recommendations I had made. But not for a moment had I anticipated this level of interest or, subsequently, the notoriety that accompanied it.

As I have mentioned previously, my political interest in matters relating to Scottish independence had become more widely known, of which more later, whilst at the same time another army officer, Eric Joyce, who was a major in the Royal Army Educational Corps (RAEC), had gained considerably more notoriety than I had by writing a piece on the evils of class structure in the army which had been published in the journal of the decidedly left-leaning Fabian Society. Joyce, of course, went on to become the Labour MP for Falkirk and an almost permanent feature in the national media, not least for his fisticuff exploits in one of the House of Commons bars which led to him being constrained and then led away by no fewer than eight of the Met's finest. Thereafter his fall from grace was pretty swift.

Nonetheless, the combination of his writing on class bias and mine on institutionalised racism in the army seemed to have frightened the horses somewhat, and the hierarchy might possibly have feared leftist infiltration and subversion in the officer corps. Whatever the reason might have been, I found myself being formally investigated by the Special Investigations Branch (SIB) of the Royal Military Police (RMP) for alleged misdemeanours the nature of which I was never quite clear about, actually.

I was summoned for an interview under caution at the SIB offices deep in the bowels of Edinburgh Castle, where I was greeted by the two Warrant Officers (WOs) who were to interrogate me. In common soldiers' parlance the RMP are usually referred to as 'the Monkeys' and I recognised two fine examples of the species. So fine, in fact, that they might have been promoted to the lofty heights of being apes. Their physical movements were slow, ponderous, and measured, and I had no doubt that their mental agility would probably be the same. I swear I could hear the whirring of their brains as they set out on their clearly pre-rehearsed routine.

I can't remember if I was required to give evidence under oath, but I do know I declined their offer of a lawyer. In retrospect I regretted this, because I could probably have had even more fun with them; a lawyer would have, I'm sure, told me to say nothing, and in the absence of anything incriminating aside from their, or their masters', suspicions they would have had nowhere to go. However I was quite happy to tell them the truth, although the truth was not necessarily what they wanted to hear.

I *knew* they wanted me to say something along the lines of; 'All right, Guv, it's a fair cop, you've caught me bang to rights. I am indeed a communist sympathiser sleeper embedded in the British military establishment, just waiting for the word from the Kremlin.' What they got, though, when they asked why I had sent a copy of my report to every organisation and individual I had consulted, was that it was a courtesy common in academic circles and not to have done so would have been extremely bad manners.

That left them completely nonplussed and dissatisfied, but it was the truth, just not the whole story, for as I have said previously my fear was that my work would disappear without trace. Ultimately I ended up getting a formal written reprimand from General Jonny Hall, my friend and mentor, who seemed to be most embarrassed by the whole affair. I recall that as I signed to acknowledge the receipt of this missive his only comment was that he couldn't possibly afford the Mont Blanc pen I was using. I don't think he was taking it seriously either!

Chapter 29

By this time I sensed the end of my military career was looming. Not only had I departed from the traditional, fast track career path at my own choosing, but I had run foul of a rotten brigade commander who had written my annual report down mainly out of spite and personal dislike. Plus my interest in politics was now bourgeoning as the independence debate in Scotland heated up, and I wanted to be in amongst that particular action. All of these things came together at more or less the same time.

My flirtation with the politics of Scottish independence had started some time before, when I had been doing my DF in Glasgow. In particular I was interested in how an independent Scotland might go about organising its defence forces if and when the time came to do so. I started writing a bit about it here and there and briefing various journalists. I did so anonymously in the main, as serving personnel were not meant to talk to the media at the time, a restriction I was to find increasingly tiresome as time wore on. In fact we weren't even meant to speak to our MPs either, which I thought was completely at odds with our rights as UK citizens.

Whilst at the university, then, and in parallel to my research into race and racism, I started – in my spare time of course – to draw up a blueprint for a hypothetical Scottish Defence Force

(SDF) post independence. There was nothing particularly radical in my approach in this early attempt; I merely applied the principles taught on all British military courses, known as the military appreciation or combat estimate, a well practised procedural and planning process to get me to what I wanted to present. It was very much carried out along conventional military lines, and the end result was pretty conventional too, and of its time. I did, however, make a couple of what in hindsight were silly and naïve mistakes, to which I will return.

So there I was at the university, halfway through my fellowship and with a completed manuscript on how I thought an independent Scotland might organise its armed forces. What to do with it now was the immediate question. So I sent it to Hew Strachan, my supervisor, and asked him what he thought. He read it and liked it, and suggested that the SCWS, his baby, could publish it as an 'occasional paper'. I was flattered, but the problem was that I couldn't put my name to it as a serving soldier given the MoD restrictions on freedom of expression. This was solved by us agreeing that it could be published under a *nom de plume,* that of Jack Hawthorn, my maternal grandfather who had sadly died before I was born.

And so it came to pass that *Some Thoughts on an Independent Scottish Defence Force,* by Jack Hawthorn, was published by Glasgow University on 1 October 1997 as Occasional Paper Number 1 by the SCWS. In fact, as far as I am aware, it remains the only occasional paper published by the institution, but I'm happy to be corrected. Anyway, it was published, which I was pleased about, albeit quietly and without fanfare. That, however, would change dramatically in due course.

At roughly the same time, in parallel and not in any deliberate or coordinated sense, I was contacted out of the blue by the SNP. They had picked up on some of the stuff I had been writing and commenting on and were keen to meet up. So I first met with their defence spokesman, a delightful former head teacher called Colin Campbell, for a coffee and a chat. Colin went on to be one of their MSPs in the reinstated Scottish Parliament in 1999 and we got on very well over the years. Politically, defence had long been the SNP's Achilles' Heel – some would say it still is – so they were interested in the views of a military professional.

At some point the question was asked if I would be interested in joining the SNP. I hadn't been a member of any political party before, although at the height of Tony Blair's 'things can only get better' New Labour I had approached his party with a general enquiry about joining them, in response to a newspaper advertisement I think. All I got back from them was a request for money, so I decided that Labour was not the party for me, thank goodness. I would never have been able to live down the shame if I had gone ahead.

The SNP was different. In those early days it was just emerging from niche interest status and was nothing like the disciplined, nay over-disciplined, behemoth of today. It was still extremely wary of what it saw as the British establishment, which as a serving army officer I was very obviously part of, and was paranoid about being infiltrated by the dark forces of the British state. So before being admitted I had to be interviewed, or perhaps vetted would be more accurate, by their then chief executive, one Mike Russell, who later went on to hold various cabinet positions when the SNP formed the administration at the Holyrood parliament.

This interview took place in the Glasgow Art Club, in Bath Street in that fair city. I wasn't aware of it at the time, but it is by all accounts 'one of Glasgow's, and Scotland's, most respected institutions', having been founded in 1867 and whose membership over the years has included some of Scotland's more famous artists. On the minus side, it only admitted women members in 1982, which probably indicates what sort of a club it was historically. Presumably Mike Russell was a member, and whatever passed between us then it must have done enough to dispel any fears that I was a member of the security services. Or, possibly, that they surmised that I *might* be a member of the security services but having met me there wasn't much to worry about. I passed.

I was then put on the party confidential list held at party HQ, together with everybody else whose job or position might be deemed to be in jeopardy because of membership of the SNP. This would include many public servants and other military individuals. Strange, though, that in a liberal western democracy this was seen as necessary. I'm pretty sure this is not the case anymore; patronage from the SNP is now an essential prerequisite for advancement in public life in Scotland, exactly as it was before from the Labour party when it held sway.

I found myself, therefore, as a very new, wet-behind-the ears, but fully fledged member of a political party for the first time in my life. My only real area of expertise was in military matters, but that just happened to be the area in which SNP expertise was lacking, to the point of non-existence. Colin Campbell was a decent chap and a good friend, but his personal knowledge of things military was close to zero. So I was it, really, as far as the party was concerned.

Not everybody was pleased with my accession. The broader membership was deeply suspicious. I was a middle class, privately educated services officer, with my kids at private school in their turn and also, Heaven forfend, with private health insurance! More than once I was asked directly if I was working for MI5, which of course I said I wasn't, but my questioners always looked far from convinced.

The first elections for the new Scottish parliament were now looming, and I was persuaded, with little resistance from me I have to say, to go through the internal vetting procedure to get on the approved candidate list. I can't remember too much about it except there were a couple of interviews and some role-playing exercises. The latter mainly featured angry, middle-aged men mouthing the current *independentista* mantras and ideology – the tyranny of the accepted orthodoxy if you like – which I'm sure they hoped would gain them candidate status, whilst I felt like a fish out of water. Nonetheless, I passed and my name was added to the list.

Then I had to find a constituency association that might take me as their candidate. I was on a very steep learning curve here, and it became clear early on that all the constituencies where there was even a ghost of a chance of an SNP win, and there weren't very many back in 1999, had been snapped up quickly. As very much a Johnny-come-lately on the scene I had to try to pick up the scraps elsewhere. So I duly applied to a few constituency associations that advertised for potential candidates and was invited to two or three for interview.

My first attempt was for the Argyll and Bute constituency, where a very young Duncan Hamilton prevailed. I then drove up to Dornoch with George Kerevan, who much later became the SNP MP for East Lothian for a while, to try for what is now the Caithness, Sutherland, and Ross constituency. Here the hustings were held in a room in a pub which was almost bisected by a fixed partition, and to address the assembled throng I had first to look round a corner one way and then the other, which was completely farcical. I was also completely flummoxed when, having delivered my bit on the importance of defence and security in an independent Scotland, a lady with a lovely soft Highland lilt said; 'Well, that's all very well, Mr Crawford, but what about the local fishing fleet?' I didn't even know there was one so I crashed and burned.

Finally, I travelled down from my home in East Lothian across the Lammermuir Hills to the Roxburgh and Berwickshire constituency to present to the party faithful there. You usually got about twenty minutes to talk and then answer questions before you were shown the door and the next victim was ushered in. So I did my bit, left, and then started to drive again, feeling like a bit of an old hand at the game by now. I had probably only gone a few miles when I received a call on this new-fangled thing called a mobile phone, and to my surprise if not astonishment I was informed that the constituency association had selected me as their candidate. Trebles all round! The truth is, delighted as I was, it was small beer really for the members were few in number and the constituency, although in my naivety I didn't realise it, was a no-hoper as far as chances of winning were concerned.

Appropriately fired up by my successful candidature, I set to with some gusto and over the following weeks and months became a frequent visitor to the area. To my mild dismay, however, I quickly realised that one half of the constituency association couldn't stand the other half, which wasn't exactly conducive to coordinated campaigning, and I had to be careful to divide my time equally between the two factions. It also became obvious that I was in traditional, deeply conservative (with a small 'c'), and entrenched Liberal Democrat territory, where the answer to every question seemed to be 'it's aye been' and where the SNP had very limited support.

On the plus side, the countryside was beautiful and I had a delightful election agent in Alex Thomson, so I had no complaints there. An added bonus was the drive back home over the Lammermuirs on the Duns to Haddington road in the early evening, with the lights just coming on as dusk was falling and Edinburgh, the Forth estuary, and Lothians in all their glory in the panoramic view presented at the top of the hill. At those moments it felt good to be alive.

On one occasion Alex Salmond, then leader of the SNP, joined me for a day's campaigning. I had never met him before but I must say I was impressed. He was hugely popular when we roamed the streets of Kelso and Hawick and passed on the one piece of electioneering advice I have never forgotten: when meeting people, he said, look them in the eyes, and if their eyes are dead move on quickly. Good advice for many other social settings too!

I was increasingly conscious that I was doing all this politicking under the radar as far as my employer, the army, was concerned. I had had a quick look at the army's rules bible, Queen's Regulations (QRs), about what I was up to and it was stated clearly that on being declared as a political candidate I was supposed to resign my commission forthwith. This presented me with a real dilemma because I had a mortgage and school fees to pay and needed to keep earning my salary right up until the last safe moment before the election. In the end the decision was taken out of my hands as I will explain shortly.

Whilst all of this was going on it started to leak out, inevitably, that I was involved with the SNP on the defence side of things, which seemed to set of a few alarm bells in the other political parties. 'An army officer in the SNP? Whoever heard of such a thing?' seemed to be the standard reaction. Just after the Christmas/New Year break in early 1999 it all came to a head. Colin Campbell, my friend and senior defence spokesman, was on his way to a seminar at Glasgow University to debate independence defence issues, very possibly hosted by the SCWS although I can't be absolutely sure, when he was informed that somebody had leaked that I was the true author of the Jack Hawthorn pamphlet which was to form the basis for much of the discussion. He passed on this news to me and advised me to adopt a low profile for a while. I'm pretty sure I know who leaked the information, but he got his own comeuppance in due course so no need to rake over the coals.

What happened next, however, was the unleashing of a tsunami of media frenzy over the following fortnight. The Labour party in particular sought to extract maximum advantage of the situation, ('weaponising the issue', I suppose we'd call it nowadays), and attack the SNP through me. A compliant and complicit Scottish political press corps duly obliged. Here my writing came back to bite me, for as I recorded earlier I had made two rather naïve mistakes in the Hawthorn paper. The first was that I had made a tongue-in-cheek comment on the Scots Guards, that fine regiment, suggesting that there could be no place for them in the SDF as they were too closely associated and integrated with the British army's Brigade of Guards. In other words, they were too British for an independent Scotland's armed forces, a comment which did not go down well with the Bufton Tuftons in the leather armchairs in their London clubs.

Second, and much more damaging politically, was that having read an article in a military journal on the utility of ballistic missiles for smaller states, I had added a couple of paragraphs in the Hawthorn paper at the very last moment prior to publication saying that they should be considered in terms of the equipment inventory. Worse still, thinking I was writing an academic paper at the time, I had mentioned that they could carry a variety of warheads including nuclear and chemical ones.

Both of these were seized upon by political opponents and media alike, and I was instantly labelled 'Colonel Calamity' by the tabloids. As the media focus intensified, I was frequently warned not to return home as there were photographers waiting in my driveway, all ten feet of it, was doorstepped in the evenings and at weekends by various journalists, and on one infamous occasion a hack from one of the more prestigious and upmarket broadsheets put my home number on constant redial and allowed it to ring continuously for half the night.

The zenith of this madness, though, was when I turned on the BBC six o'clock news and found that I was lead item on it, supported by a photograph of me that I had never seen before. I actually *do* know who leaked that one, for it was clearly taken during my time at Army HQ Scotland and I understand *exactly* how it got to the BBC. I have yet to take my revenge, but I have not forgotten, and when the time comes the swiftness and ferocity of my ire will be awesome to behold, I promise.

Anyway, against this frenetic background, the army quite understandably raised a collective eyebrow and expressed mild concern. There was just no escape from the coverage. Army HQ Scotland seemed to be paralysed and without a clue how it should react, so I thought it was high time for a conversation with the personnel folk at the MoD. I made the call and had a longish chat with the staff officer there in which I laid my cards out on the table, so to speak, and noted that I thought QRs said I should resign my commission straight away.

And here there unfolded another occasion when my faith in the system was restored. My correspondent first said that QRs were absolutely clear on the matter and that I should resign, but actually they were quite relaxed about it all. So, he went on, why didn't I just wait until four weeks before the date of the election before doing so, thereby sustaining my outgoings right up until the last safe moment? And, while we were at it, if I were for any reason to be an unsuccessful candidate (how kind!), why didn't I just rejoin the army afterwards? Apparently they were happy that I could keep my rank and seniority and just continue with my career almost as if nothing had happened. Having that safety net was hugely reassuring and I have never forgotten how benevolently I was treated.

So that's what I did. And once again the MoD played a blinder, because I wrote formally and said that I wanted to leave the army on 1 April 1999, as that was the date I had joined 4th Tanks back in 1980 and also because I thought it mildly amusing to pack it all in on April Fool's Day. Not long after I got yet another phone call from the MoD, and was told that whilst they appreciated the joke it would be much better for me personally if I changed my resignation date to 6 April as that guaranteed me another year's pension entitlement. I thanked them profusely and rather meekly changed the date as advised.

And then the last few weeks of electioneering were upon us, and passed in a paroxysm of activity, leafleting here, putting in an appearance there, and sometimes getting a photograph in the local press. Every political candidate at some point contracts 'candidatitis', a state of mild hysteria which persuades them that they might actually have a chance of winning. I was not an exception to this phenomenon but was brought crashing back down to earth at the count, as so many are. The very affable Lib Dem candidate, Euan Robson, won by a country mile.

Seeing my obvious disappointment, Euan was very magnanimous in his victory and spoke kindly to me on the platform where we gave our post election speeches. I did manage to poll 4,719 votes in total, a number I will never forget, which I thought was a poor show at the time but now realise was not too bad for a first attempt, unknown candidate in a no hope constituency. We did manage to beat the Labour party into fourth place, which was a victory of sorts I suppose. All of the candidates in Roxburgh and Berwickshire, though, got on just fine with one another and there was zero nastiness or point-scoring between us.

Waking up the next morning, late, as the count had been declared in the early hours of the morning, I realised I now had to decide what to do next, and quickly. Should I take up the MoD's offer and return to uniform, or should I seek to boldly go where no man had gone before? (I exaggerate here for effect, lots of people had done it before me.) On reflection I decided that once I had left the army I had left the army and there was no going back, so despite being deeply committed financially in family matters, I took what a friend called at the time 'a decision of extraordinary boldness' and confirmed both my retiral from 4th Tanks and the resignation of my commission.

Chapter 30

Having made the decision I now had to exit the army. In those days the resettlement arrangements were fairly generous; a few weeks' resettlement leave, a resettlement grant, and various courses you could go on to sort out a job, accommodation, and so on.

You could also, if you were of pensionable age, commute part of your pension entitlement and take it as a lump sum, which then led to your annual pension entitlement being adjusted accordingly until you reached the magic age of fifty-five, at which point it reverted back to full value! I'm pretty sure that this doesn't happen any more, but I did take out, I think, about £70,000 to help with the purchase of my first proper house, and very grateful I was for being able to do so.

I spent my resettlement grant on a bit of media training from some ex-army chancers who I now know were bluffers and winging it, as they say, but it gave me the basics and a bit of experience of being interviewed on camera which came in handy in later years. As for the resettlement course I attended in Fife, the less said the better. It was outsourced by the MoD to a bunch who called themselves the Career Transition Partnership (CTP) and was appallingly poor. Most of the time was spent on writing your *curriculum vitae,* but many of us had done that already. There wasn't much else about it that was any good so I baled out early. I sincerely hope that it's light years better nowadays.

What I did discover very quickly, however, was that the most difficult thing of all in transitioning back into civvy street and getting a job was deciding what I wanted to do. All my training as a combat arms officer in the army had been generalist in nature. I could attack any hill you liked in multiple ways. I had organised parades and formal dinners and parties, escorted journalists and VIP visitors, written for and edited magazines and journals, taught at staff college, flown the flag for Britain abroad, and many other things. Any officer worth his salt, if asked to escort three nuns and a kangaroo to Outer Mongolia, would just get on with it and generally do it well.

But in civvy street, I discovered, that all mattered little. You might have planned and carried out the Normandy landings single-handedly, but if you couldn't point to five years' experience working in a call centre you were never going to get that manager's job that was going there. I had done many great and wonderful things in my military career, but none of them had involved the raising of cash or the generation of revenue through commerce. In short, potential employers were unable to see how hiring me, at the relatively advanced age of forty-five, would help their bottom line. Here was a frustration I shared with many other ex-services personnel seeking entry to the jobs market.

I must have applied for literally hundreds of jobs. Positions were usually advertised in the newspapers, this being before widespread internet use and online job posting became the norm, so countless letters, cvs, and envelopes went through my printer and off to multiple organisations who I thought would be bowled over by my experience and skills set. Nothing could have been further from the truth, and it was an unsettling introduction to the harsh world of the civilian jobs market.

I did manage to get a few interviews, but the vast majority of responses to my applications were rejections, or many times no reply at all, which I thought and still do think was terribly rude. Then, on one infamous occasion, I was offered a job on the spot after an interview with an extremely well known PR and communications agency on a Friday afternoon, only for the founder and chief executive to phone me on the following Monday to say he had changed his mind. It transpired that he had spoken to a prominent Scottish journalist over the weekend to get a second opinion, and for reasons never explained she had clearly put the boot in. (Names are available on application for those interested.)

This was a blow, because whilst not exactly desperate (thank you again, army pension) I had been searching fruitlessly for a few months by then. At this low point I wasn't really sure what I should do next. Friends were very supportive, and the best bit of advice I got came from ex-4 RTR chum Richard Hickson, who told me that I would definitely get a job at some point but no-one could predict when that might be. I have passed on that little gem to others many times since.

Another phenomenon of the time was ex-military people, some of whom I didn't know at all, inviting me to visit them at their places of work for a coffee and a chat about job hunting. At first I thought this was very kind, but then realised that in fact most of them were saying 'come and look at how well I have done'. Nobody, but nobody, had either the clout or inclination to actually offer me a job, not even as an unpaid, work experience, intern type of person, which was deeply disappointing. The fact was that for all their bluster and promises they were just as powerless as I was, the difference being of course that they had paid employment and I did not.

Desperate days called for desperate measures, and I had a rethink. If nobody was prepared to employ me, I thought, then I would just have to employ myself. I had run a couple of my own small businesses when I was a student so the concept of being self-employed wasn't completely alien to me, but now having to support a family brought a whole new dimension to the prospect. Nonetheless I started, as I have done so many times before and since, from first principles. In the centre of a plain sheet of paper I drew a circle with the word 'me' inside it (I hasten to add I was not trying to portray myself as the centre of the Universe).

From this circle I drew a few lines outwards to designate the areas in which I was most interested in working, namely defence, politics, and journalism. Next, I attached the names of the people I knew who worked in those sectors to the relevant string, and finally, in an act of supreme anal retentiveness, I colour coded it. It resulted in a sort of job-seeking mind map, and I suppose I could have done the same thing using a Venn diagram if I had thought about it. But now I had a visual picture of who did what, where they overlapped, and how I might pursue a more targeted attempt to get a job.

After a cursory examination of my new chart the term 'political lobbyist' leapt out at me. I had no real knowledge of what a political lobbyist actually did, but I could have a good guess, and it struck me that the combination of interests in defence, politics, and journalism might perhaps make me useful to, say, a company operating in the defence industries that needed a political and media communications programme without having the bother of recruiting someone to do it in-house.

After reconstructing my cv and covering letter to appeal better to what I thought might be would-be employers of political lobbyists, I sent copies to the two or three people who had been really helpful in past applications and just asked them whether they thought I was on the right track. The answer was unanimously and resoundingly in the affirmative, which was encouraging.

I then had the thought that, in addition to hoping that defence industries might hire me as a consultant, PR companies could possibly be interested in adding some general political expertise to their offering, especially since the Scottish parliament was by then up and running. I thought that perhaps two or three of them might consider taking on someone like me on a one or two days per week basis. Accordingly, as one did in those days, I looked up all the PR companies in Edinburgh in the Yellow Pages and sent them my cv with a covering letter explaining the benefits I could bring in knowledge and expertise and, crucially, also to their bottom line.

Nothing happened for a bit, and then in one of those right person, right time, right place coincidences my letter landed on the desk of the managing director of one of the PR companies whose major client had just asked him how they planned to brief them on the new Scottish political context and what was going on in the parliament at Holyrood. I was therefore called in for interview as I offered an instant solution to his new problem, and after a quick chat about things in general and what I could do for them I was hired as a self-employed consultant on a two day per week basis, which later rose to three days. Sighs of relief all round.

The icing on the cake was that their client in need of political intelligence was none other than Motorola, at that time the biggest private sector employer in Scotland. Alas, it lasted only a few months until the company took the decision to close their operation, throwing hundreds into unemployment. However it set me on my way, and twenty years of being a freelance lobbyist and writer was to follow.

But that's a completely separate story.

Afternote

Twenty plus years on from leaving the army people still ask me if I regret leaving. It's a difficult question to answer, to be honest, because the true context is a time when I was younger and so were all of my friends and comrades, and they have all left too. Some of them, sadly, have passed on to the big tank leaguer in the sky.

A better question might be 'Would you do it all again?', to which the answer is a definite yes, but with caveats. I would do it all over again if I were the same young, fit person I was at twenty-six when I joined 4 RTR. But I would have to be with the same people at the same age, and in the same places at the times we visited them. I had the great good fortune to serve alongside fine young officers and outstanding NCOs and men, so if they were all restored as they were then nothing would give me greater pleasure than to repeat the whole experience.

Do I have any regrets? A few, but none that keep me awake at night. I wish I had enjoyed Sandhurst instead of hating it, but I went there having worked for three years in a civvy job as a trainee chartered surveyor and with no previous military experience whatsoever, so I think hating it was understandable. Much of the training there had seemed ridiculous and pointless to me. I was, however, very conscious that my Dad had done it in 1946 and if he could do it then so could I. Not that he leaned on me in any way.

I wish I had realised that my time as a young troop leader in Germany was as absolutely glorious as it was and would never be repeated. Youth is wasted on the young as we all know, but apart from my time at Millfield School in Somerset, being a subaltern was without doubt (birth of my three children excepted) the best time in my life, ever. Nothing else compares. I have never since experienced that combination of elation and delight when I led my tank troop out down the Rattlesnake Road in Canada, or when we beat up the mess in Munster and Tidworth in the aftermath of some dinner night or impromptu event. Nobody else I knew in civvy street had as much fun as we did.

I should have pursued my desire to train as a helicopter pilot with the AAC with a bit more vigour, and shouldn't have allowed myself to be blindsided and bamboozled by a selfish RTR officer plan into not doing it. That was a mistake. And very possibly I might have been better resigning my commission a few years earlier to give me a softer landing in civvy street, but who knows? And that's it, really, everything else was fine.

What I did realise in the latter part of my service was that, to get ahead, you really did have to buckle down and not rock the boat. Having always been a bit of a dissenter and questioner of norms I think the writing was on the wall as soon as the phrase 'a bit of a maverick' appeared in one of my annual confidential reports. I hope that nobody actively disliked me for being a bit of an iconoclast, but I'm sure more than a few disapproved of me and the way I went about the business of being a career army officer. The peacetime British army tends to select in its own image, as many other organisations do too, but I was in very few personal images of those above me at the end!

That said, I will be eternally grateful to the army for giving me the chance to work alongside the most professionally competent, irreverent, and humorous bunch of individuals I could ever have wished for. The friendships have lasted right up to this day, and are closer and deeper than those which might be forged in most civvy organisations I am sure. You could argue that we all know far too much about each other, but you could also argue that this allows us to look after each other better and more compassionately as we all get older. And it will go on and on until there aren't any of us left.

I wouldn't have missed it for the world.

Glossary

1 (Br) Corps	1st (British) Corps
4RTR	4th Royal Tank Regiment
5 INNIS DG	5th Iniskilling Dragoon Guards
7 Armd Bde	7th Armoured Brigade
12 Armd Bde	12th Armoured Brigade
9/12 L	9th/12th Lancers
17/21 L	17th/21st Lancers
AAC	Army Air Corps
ADC	Aide-de-camp
ADF	Australian Defence Force
APWT	Annual personal weapon test
ARV	Armoured recovery vehicle
ASC	Army Staff College
BAOR	British Army of the Rhine
BAR	British Army Review
BARITWE	Best Armoured Regiment in the World Ever
BATUS	British Army Training Unit Suffield
BCR	Battle casualty replacement
BDA	Battle damage assessment
BEF	British Expeditionary Force
BFES	British Families Education Service
BFPO	British Forces Post Office

BG	Battlegroup
BMH	British Military Hospital
BV	Boiling vessel
CCF	Combined Cadet Force
CEUOTC	City of Edinburgh Universities Officers' Training Corps
CGS	Chief of the General Staff
CILOR	Cash in lieu of rations
CO	Commanding Officer
Compo	Composite rations
COS	Chief of Staff
CRE	Commission for Racial Equality
CTP	Career Transition Partnership
CVR(T)	Combat Vehicle Reconnaisance (Tracked)
DAMCON	Damage control
DCOS	Deputy Chief of Staff
DF	Defence Fellowship
DLI	Durham Light Infantry
D&M	Driving and maintenance
DP	Displaced person
DS	Directing staff
DSACEUR	Deputy Supreme Allied Commander Europe
DST	Discarding sabot training
FSC	Ferret scout car
FTX	Field training exercise
GCNG	Greek Cypriot National Guard
GMP	Greater Manchester Police
GOC	General Officer Commanding
GPS	Global positioning system

HBMGC	Heavy Branch of the Machine Gun Corps
HLI	Highland Light Infantry
HQDRAC	Headquarters of the Director Royal Armoured Corps
IFV	Infantry fighting vehicle
IGB	Inner German border
ITDU	Infantry Trials and Development Unit
JDSC	Junior Division of Staff College
JSCSC	Joint Services Command and Staff College
KCI	Kansas City International airport
KOSB	King's Own Scottish Borderers
KTO	Kuwait Theatre of Operations
LAV	Light armoured vehicle
LG	Life Guards
LOA	Local overseas allowance
MA	Military Assistant
MBT	Main battle tank
MILAN	Milan anti-tank guided missile
MoD	Ministry of Defence
MQ	Married quarter
MSO	Mixed services organisation
MT	Motor transport
NBC	Nuclear, biological and chemical
NCO	Non-commissioned officer
NT	National Trust
OC	Officer commanding
OTC	Officers' Training Corps
PAC	Pakistan Armoured Corps
PIA	Pakistan International Airlines

PJHQ	Permanent Joint Headquarters
POR	Post operational report
PPL	Private pilot's licence
QARANC	Queen Alexandra's Royal Army Nursing Corps
QM	Quartermaster
QM (Tech)	Quartermaster (Technical)
QOHldrs	Queen's Own Highlanders
QRs	Queen's Regulations
QRIH	Queen's Royal Irish Hussars
RA	Royal Artillery
RAC	Royal Armoured Corps
RAEC	Royal Army Educational Corps
RAMC	Royal Army Medical Corps
RAOC	Royal Army Ordnance Corps
RCB	Regular Commissions Board
RE	Royal Engineers
Rebro	Rebroadcast
REME	Royal Electrical and Mechanical Engineers
RFA	Royal Fleet Auxiliary
RGO	Regimental Gunnery Officer
RHG/D	Blues and Royals
RIR	Royal Irish Rifles
RGFC	Republican Guard Force Command
RHQ	Regimental Headquarters
RLC	Royal Logistic Corps
RMAS	Royal Military Academy Sandhurst
RMCS	Royal Military College of Science
RMP	Royal Military Police

RNAZ	Royal New Zealand Air Force
RQMS	Regimental Quartermaster Sergeant
RSO	Regimental Signals Officer
RTC	Royal Tank Corps
SBA	Sovereign Base Area
Scots DG	Royal Scots Dragoon Guards
SCUD	SCUD ballistic missile
SCWS	Scottish Centre for War Studies
SDF	Scottish Defence Forces
SHQ	Squadron Headquarters
SIB	Special Investigations Branch
SIM	Simulator
SIS	Secret Intelligence Service
SLR	Self loading rifle
SMG	Sterling submachine gun
SP	Strathclyde Police
SQMS	Squadron Quartermaster Sergeant
SSC	Short service commission
SSM	Squadron Sergeant Major
Stag	To be on sentry duty
SY	Scottish Yeomanry
TA	Territorial Army
TAOR	Tactical area of responsibilty
TI	Thermal imaging
TLS	Tank laser sight
TRNC	Turkish Republic of Northern Cyprus
UAS	University Air Squadron
UN	United Nations
UOR	Urgent operational requirement

USACGSC	US Army Command and General Staff College
VFR	Visual flight rules
VHF	Very high frequency
VOR	Vehicle off the road
WAGs	Wives and girlfriends
WFM	Whole fleet management
WOSB	War Office Selection Board